RODALE ORGANIC **GARDENING BASICS**

W9-CCD-509

perennials

RODALE

**From the Editors of
Rodale Organic Gardening
Magazine and Books**

RODALE

WE **INSPIRE** AND **ENABLE** PEOPLE TO IMPROVE
THEIR LIVES AND THE WORLD AROUND THEM

© 2001 by Rodale Inc.

All rights reserved. No part of this publication may be reproduced or transmitted in any form or by any means, electronic or mechanical, including photocopy, recording, or any other information storage and retrieval system, without the written permission of the publisher.

The information in this book has been carefully researched, and all efforts have been made to ensure accuracy. Rodale Inc. assumes no responsibility for any injuries suffered or for damages or losses incurred during the use of or as a result of following this information. It's important to study all directions carefully before taking any action based on the information and advice presented in this book. When using any commercial product, *always* read and follow label directions. Where trade names are used, no discrimination is intended and no endorsement by Rodale Inc. is implied.

Printed in the United States of America on acid-free ∞, recycled ♻ paper

We're always happy to hear from you. For questions or comments concerning the editorial content of this book, please write to:

Rodale Book Readers' Service
33 East Minor Street
Emmaus, PA 18098

Look for other Rodale books wherever books are sold. Or call us at (800) 848-4735.

For more information about Rodale Organic Gardening magazine and books, visit us at:

www.organicgardening.com

Editor: Christine Bucks
Interior Book Designer: Nancy Smola Biltcliff
Cover Designer: Patricia Field
Cover Photographer: Clive Nichols
Photography Editor: Lyn Horst
Photography Assistant: Jackie L. Ney
Layout Designer: Dale Mack
Researchers: Diana Erney and
    Sarah Wolfgang Heffner
Copy Editors: Pamela Angulo and Stacey A. Follin
Manufacturing Coordinator: Patrick T. Smith
Indexer: Nan N. Badgett
Editorial Assistance: Kerrie A. Cadden

RODALE ORGANIC GARDENING BOOKS
Executive Editor: Kathleen DeVanna Fish
Managing Editor: Fern Marshall Bradley
Executive Creative Director: Christin Gangi
Art Director: Patricia Field
Production Manager: Robert V. Anderson Jr.
Studio Manager: Leslie M. Keefe
Copy Manager: Nancy N. Bailey
Manufacturing Manager: Eileen Bauder

**Library of Congress
    Cataloging-in-Publication Data**
    Rodale organic gardening basics. Volume 6, Perennials / from the editors of Rodale organic gardening magazine and books.
        p.   cm.
    Includes bibliographical references (p.   ) and index.
    ISBN 0-87596-855-4 (pbk. : alk. paper)
    1. Perennials.   2. Organic gardening.
I. Title: Perennials.   II. Rodale Books.
III. Organic gardening (Emmaus, Pa. : 1988)
IV. Rodale organic gardening basics ; v. 6.
SB434 .R59   2001
635.9'3284—dc21   00-009601

Distributed in the book trade by St. Martin's Press

2 4 6 8 10 9 7 5 3 1   paperback

The Joy of Growing Perennials

Nature's greatest gifts to the home gardener are perennials—bouquets of beautiful flowers that last and last. And while growing perennials may seem like a challenge if you're a beginning gardener, getting them to grace your beds season after season really isn't difficult. That said, here are five simple "secrets" of perennials that reveal why you'll want to start planting them today:

Perennials are practically care-free, and they'll come back every year—same time, same place.

1. Perennials are practically care-free. Dig a hole in the ground, stick them in, and watch them grow! They'll come back every year—same time, same place.

2. As perennials spread, you can divide them and get more free plants to fill in your garden.

3. You don't need to fertilize perennials if you plant them in soil that you've amended with compost.

4. Planting perennials will invite good bugs such as lady beetles to hang out in your garden.

5. The more perennials you have in your garden, the less work you'll have to do. For example, you won't have to replant things year after year.

Of course, the best reason to plant perennials is for pure indulgence: to be able to stroll through your garden and enjoy their fragrance and magical beauty. Once you begin growing your own, I'm sure you'll agree that few things in life are as pleasurable as perennials.

Happy organic gardening!

Maria Rodale

Perennials will give you a lush show year after year in return for very little work on your part.

chapter one

Go Organic: Growing Perennials Simplified

Growing perennials can be tremendously rewarding. After all, isn't it great to sit in your backyard and enjoy the beautiful work of art you've created? Or to decorate your home with vases of freshly cut flowers—or share colorful bouquets with friends?

ORGANIC = EASY

Of course, you might think that to grow such wonderful masterpieces you'd need to use chemicals, and lots of them. But you couldn't be further from the truth. You don't need to use *any* chemicals to grow perennials. In fact, just by gardening organically and following good gardening practices, you'll create a natural balance between the soil, your plants, and insects that results in healthy plants. Which means the time you'll have saved by *not* applying chemicals will give you more time to spend smelling the flowers.

You don't need to use any chemicals to grow perennials.

6 THINGS YOU CAN STOP DOING NOW

No matter whether you've grown perennials before or are trying it for the first time, check out this list of things you can *stop* doing when you grow perennials the organic way.

1. STOP Using Chemicals!

The best gardens start with healthy soil, and your soil's health will improve as soon as you stop using pesticides, herbicides, and synthetic fertilizers. If you put chemicals on your garden, they'll leach into the soil and possibly harm the beneficial insects—"the good guys"—and helpful microorganisms that live there.) If you garden organically, the natural organisms will return. And as an added bonus, you won't have to worry about chemicals potentially harming you, your family, or your pets.

2. STOP **Keeping a Messy Garden!**

Weeding is an important aspect of any type of gardening, whether it be edible or ornamental. That's because weeds can crowd plants, while weed roots compete with other plant roots for food and water. If you devote just a few minutes a day to weeding, you'll be much better off than if you let weeds take over your garden and then try to regain control with a marathon weeding session.

3. STOP **Killing Every Caterpillar You Find!**

When you see a caterpillar inching up a stem of one of your prized plants, your first instinct may be to

Pull weeds when they're small to give your perennials a competitive edge in the garden.

squash it. But not every bug in your garden is a "bad guy." Lots of good guys hang out there, too—and they may actually help your garden. So, the next time you see a caterpillar in your garden, take some time to identify it to see if it should be left unharmed.

4. STOP Overfertilizing!

If you've prepared your soil well before planting, your perennials probably won't need more than an application of compost in the middle of the season to grow vigorously. Overfertilizing is not only a waste of your time and of resources, but can also give your perennials too much of a boost, making them grow tall and spindly.

PERENNIALS KEY WORDS

Perennial plant. A plant that flowers and sets seed for two or more seasons. Short-lived perennials like coreopsis and columbines may live 3 to 5 years; long-lived perennials like peonies may live 100 years or more.

Tender perennial. A perennial plant from tropical or subtropical regions that won't survive the winter outside, except in subtropical regions such as Florida and southern California. Most gardeners grow tender perennials (which include wax begonias and coleus) as annuals.

Hardy perennial. A perennial plant that tolerates frost. Because hardy perennials vary in the degree of cold they can tolerate, make sure a plant is hardy in your USDA Hardiness Zone (see the map on page 106 to find your zone) before you buy it.

Herbaceous perennial. A perennial plant that dies back to the ground at the end of each growing season. Most garden perennials fall into this category.

Semiwoody perennial. A perennial plant that forms woody stems but is much less substantial than a shrub. Russian sage is one example of a semiwoody perennial.

Woody perennial. A perennial plant such as a shrub or tree that doesn't die down to the ground each year.

Put some thought into what you want before you buy, and you'll spend your money wisely.

Always plant perennials in sites that will meet their needs. Hostas (below), for example, love shade.

5. STOP Buying without Thinking!

Before you head out to the garden center or pick up a mail-order catalog, *think.* Think about your landscape, soil conditions, and the way you plan to use perennials in your garden. Some questions to consider are these: Do you have lots of sun or shade? Do you have soggy soil, or do you need plants for dry sites? Do you want plants with beautiful blooms, or plants with fabulous foliage? If you put some thought into what you want to buy before you shop, you'll end up coming home with the best plants for your growing conditions and for the garden style you desire.

WHAT ABOUT BULBS?

BULBS ARE a diverse group of perennial plants. They're categorized as true bulbs, corms, rhizomes, tubers, and tuberous roots—all of which are structures that store nutrients to support growth and bloom. Because some of the perennials covered in Chapter 5 grow from bulbs, you'll probably find these definitions helpful.

True bulb. True bulbs, like onions, have layers of food-storing scales surrounding the central leaves and flowering stem. The bulbs are often covered with a papery skin called a tunic. Daffodils, lilies, and hyacinths are true bulbs.

Corm. A corm is a rounded, swollen stem covered with a papery tunic. Unlike true bulbs, corms are solid, with a bud on top that produces leaves and flowers. Crocuses and gladioli are corms.

Rhizome. Rhizomes masquerade as roots but actually are thick, horizontal stems. Roots grow from the bottom of the rhizome; leaves and flowers sprout from the top. Calla lilies, cannas, and bearded irises have rhizomes.

Tuber. Tubers are fleshy underground stems that have eyes or buds from which leaves and flowers grow. Some tubers, such as caladiums and tuberous begonias, are cormlike. But tubers, unlike corms, sprout roots from the sides and top in addition to the bottom. Other tubers are woody, like anemones.

Tuberous root. Tuberous roots are swollen, fleshy roots. They have a pointed bud on top and roots that sprout from the bottom. Dahlias have tuberous roots.

6. STOP **Planting without Planning!**

Although many perennials are easy to grow, they won't do well if you plant them in a site that doesn't meet their needs. So, read up on plant requirements, then do the right thing: Plant shade lovers like hostas and astilbes out of full sun, and give sun worshippers like asters a shade-free spot. (If you have some problem areas in your yard, see our "Tough Plants for Tough Places" suggestions on page 20. If you already know which perennials you like, find out whether their needs fit your garden in the "Plant Particulars" for each of the 50 plant listings in Chapter 5.)

Having the right tools on hand when you garden makes planting and tending perennials quick and easy work.

chapter two

Tools & Supplies

One of the best things about growing perennials is that you don't need a lot of tools—even if you're just getting started. A few key items, along with some supplies (such as compost and mulch), are enough to help you create the perennial garden of your dreams.

QUALITY MATTERS

Although you don't need a lot of tools to grow a wonderful perennial garden, you should make sure that whatever you buy is well made. That's because tools are like clothes; cheap ones wear out fast, but good ones last. Plus, good tools make work easier and faster. Having a spade break off in the middle of planting is a high price to pay for choosing a shoddy tool in the first place.

Here are some features to look for—and others to avoid—when you're tool shopping.

Handles. Top-quality tools usually have handles of ash or hickory. Wooden handles are strong, durable, and feel good in your hands. Over time, wooden handles wear slightly, becoming smoother where you hold the handle. Pass on tools that have painted handles, which can hide cheap wood, and handles with visible knots, which can weaken the wood.

Sockets. Heavy-duty digging tools should have what's called solid-socket or solid-strapped construction, which places less stress on the tool head.

Blades. The working end of digging and cultivating tools should be one solid piece of rust-resistant metal, such as carbon steel. Most good carbon steel blades are half-painted, so you can see the steel on the "business end" of the tool. Avoid tools with completely painted blades; they're usually cheaply made.

6 Essential Tools
- **Garden fork**
- **Hand cultivator**
- **Trowel**
- **Spade**
- **Pruning shears**
- **Knife**

Size. Tools should work with you, not against you. So before you buy a tool, pick it up and go through the motions of using it. The tool should feel comfortable in your hands, and you shouldn't feel any strain in your neck or back.

HAND TOOLS

Hand tools form the basis of a good garden tool collection. If you keep them sharp, good-quality hand tools will make the work in your perennial beds go quickly and easily.

Trowel

A wide, sturdy trowel with a comfortable grip is indispensable for digging around established plants, digging up weeds and small plants, and transplanting small perennials. A well-designed trowel won't bend or break when you exert pressure on it.

Trowel

Spade

A spade has a flat blade with squared edges (unlike a shovel, which has a scooped blade with a rounded edge that comes to a point). Use a spade for digging planting holes and new garden beds.

Spade

Garden Fork

Wonderful for loosening soil, removing stones, and lifting and dividing perennials, a garden fork has thick, square, fairly blunt-tipped tines.

Garden fork

Pruning Shears

Although you can use a sharp pair of scissors to cut many flowers in a perennial garden, you'll need hand pruners to cut thick-stemmed blooms, such as peonies. Hand pruners are also great for removing diseased branches, taking cuttings, and trimming stakes to size. Choose the bypass (scissors) style of pruning shears, which cuts stems neatly, rather than the anvil type, which mashes stems against its flat blade.

Bypass shears

Hand Cultivator

This tool looks similar to a claw. Its small size and three tines makes it perfect for shallowly disturbing the soil between perennials, uprooting weed seedlings. It's also useful for scratching amendments into the soil around the base of a plant.

Hand cultivator

Knife

A sharp knife is essential for cutting through roots when you're dividing perennials. It works especially well for perennials likes astilbes and peonies whose crown (the part of the plant where the stem meets the roots) is pretty solid, as compared to coneflowers, which are a more loosely knit plant.

Knife

WAYS TO WATER

With a few exceptions, perennials like consistently (and preferably evenly) moist soil. So, when the top couple of inches of the soil dry out and Mother Nature isn't cooperating, you'll need to step in to quench your perennials' thirst.

quick tip

When you're working in your garden, you'll want hand tools at the ready. It helps to keep tools in some type of caddy. You can improvise one from an old bucket, and just stick all your tools inside of it. Or, you can buy a tool caddy made out of fabric. Fabric caddies contain individual pockets for your tools, and they usually fit around a 5-gallon bucket. That way, you can sit on top of the bucket (provided you still have the lid) while working, and your tools will be at your fingertips.

Watering Cans

Always water newly transplanted plants by hand, which is where a watering can comes in handy. Use a rose attachment on the spout to break the water into a fine shower, and water the soil, not the plant's leaves.

Hoses

Soaker hoses are ideal for perennial beds because you don't have to disturb the plants or beds when you water. Just lay down a soaker hose after you plant your bed, or snake it between plants in an established bed. Mulch over the hoses, and you have an invisible but very effective watering system. Soaker hoses save water and keep plant leaves dry, which helps avoid or eliminate disease problems.

Some soaker hoses ooze water over their entire length, while others spurt water through tiny holes. If you use a soaker hose with holes, be sure to face the holes downward so that water doesn't squirt up in the air like a sprinkler.

Give your perennials consistently moist soil with a watering can (top) or a soaker hose (bottom).

If you have individual plants that need a good watering but are difficult to reach with a watering can, use a regular **garden hose** with a **watering wand** attachment. A watering wand is an extension around 3 feet long that you screw onto the nozzle end of your hose.

PLANT SUPPORTS

Perennials with tall flower spikes (such as delphiniums) or full, heavy flowers (such as peonies) are especially prone to toppling. And that's where supports come in. Of course, the kind of support you choose depends on the type of flowers you're supporting. Remember, you want to see the flowers in your beds, not the support.

Individual Plant Stakes

A tall, slender branch, a slender bamboo cane, or a dark-green plastic cane is a good option to use for perennials with tall, slender bloom stalks (such as foxgloves). The best way to attach the bloom stalk to the stake is with a loop, so you don't put pressure on the stem or even cut or snap it off as it grows. Wrap soft string, yarn, or a fabric strip around the stem; turn it to form a loop or circle; then tie it to the stake. As the stem grows taller, you can add more ties as needed to keep the plant upright.

Circular Frames

Bushy perennials, such as peonies and chrysanthemums, are best supported with a circular plant frame. These frames are circles of wire with three or four wire legs that hold the entire plant upright. You could also make your own circular frame by putting four stakes around the plant and connecting the stakes with string.

The stake for this lily has a loop on it to support the plant's stalk; you could also use a slender branch and make your own loop out of yarn.

Peonies, which are bushy plants, do best with the support of a circular frame.

If you amend your perennial beds with compost before you plant, you probably won't need to add any other fertilizer.

COMPOST

Compost is the end result of heaping together waste materials, such as grass clippings and kitchen scraps. It's a gardener's black gold—the perfect soil amendment and plant fertilizer. Compost increases the soil's ability to retain moisture; improves the soil's texture, allowing roots to penetrate the soil more easily; and converts soil nutrients to a form more easily taken up by plants. Its low nitrogen content provides the right amount of nourishment for perennials. In fact, if you prepare your garden bed well before planting, compost should be the only fertilizer your perennials will need.

MULCH

Mulch is a great garden problem solver. It conserves water, keeps down weeds, adds humus and some nutrients to the soil as it breaks down, and keeps soil and nutrients from washing away during hard rains. The best mulches for perennial gardens include

- compost
- grass clippings
- shredded leaves
- newspaper
- pine needles
- straw
- shredded wood or bark chips

Don't overlook regional materials when you're choosing a mulch. For example, cocoa hulls and peanut shells make excellent, attractive mulches that can be quite affordable if they're readily available in your area.

Although it certainly makes sense to use a mulch that you have available, attractiveness is another quality to consider when choosing a mulch for your perennial garden. If you choose to a use a mulch that's not very attractive, such as newspaper, try covering it with a layer of a more appealing mulch, such as a thick layer of shredded leaves or shredded bark chips.

quick tip

Although sawdust might seem like a good organic mulch for your perennial beds, it's not. Sawdust is unattractive, it's often splintery and hard to work through, and it steals soil nitrogen from your perennials as it breaks down, causing poor plant growth.

GARDEN GLOVES

NO GARDENER should be without a good pair of gloves—even if you don't mind getting dirt under your fingernails. Gloves can prevent blisters on your hands when you're doing a lot of digging and they can keep your hands warm and dry when you're gardening in soggy weather. Wearing gloves is also a good idea when you're working around thorny plants.

Gloves come in all kinds of styles, materials, and colors. You can buy gloves made out of leather (cowhide, goatskin, or pigskin), or rubber- or plastic-coated gloves made out of cotton. Some gloves are lined with insulation, some have ribbed cuffs, and others have elasticized wrists (to keep your hands extra clean).

You'll find gloves readily available at your local garden center, home supply store, or in mail-order catalogs. (If you're not sure what size you wear, you're probably better off buying your first pair of gloves at a store, instead of through mail order, so that you can try them on and see how they fit.)

With a bit of planning, you can create a pretty and harmonious mix of perennials that are well suited to your landscape.

chapter three

Planning for Perennials

Sure, you can plant a garden without a plan. But a little bit of planning goes a long way in helping you create a garden that's truly a reflection of your tastes—as well as one that matches plants to your landscape's growing conditions. So take some time to read over the planning hints in this chapter, and then get busy!

LANDSCAPING TIPS

Perennials are all-purpose plants—you can grow them wherever you garden and in any part of your garden. But before you start buying and planting willy-nilly, ask yourself what you want out of your garden. Do you want a big garden, or just one or two small beds? Do you want to have pretty blooms only in summer, or throughout the entire growing season? Lots of flowers to cut for fresh arrangements, or a garden to enjoy mainly outside? Tour your property and determine where you have space for plantings. You can use perennials effectively in a number of ways—in borders or beds, as specimens or in mixed plantings. Then, determine the soil, moisture, and sunlight conditions of each area and select the plants whose requirements match (for starters, see "Tough Plants for Tough Places" on page 20).

You can grow perennials wherever you garden and in any part of your garden.

Perennials in Borders

If you have a fairly long area that could use some color, like the side of your house or garage, then you might want to consider planting a perennial border. To build a border, simply group plants with similar requirements for soil, moisture, and sunlight. You should also keep color combinations, height, form, and texture in mind.

Perennials in Beds

Another way to use perennials is in beds. A bed is different from a border in that it's freestanding, without an immediate background, like a fence or wall. Try beds to add color and drama to the sides of a path or to define the edge of a patio or deck. If you have a large lawn, try creating an island bed in it to relieve all that green with a bright splash of color. (If you go with an island bed, plant the tallest plants in the center of the bed, using progressively shorter plants toward the edge.)

Perennials as Specimen Plants

Larger perennials, such as peonies, make striking displays when planted alone. You can use them in the landscape wherever you want an accent but don't want to feature something as large or heavy-looking as a shrub or tree. You can also use specimen plants to mark the beginning of a path or to set off other features of your yard.

The bright purple petals of Siberian iris add a splash of color to perennial beds in spring and early summer.

Perennials in Mixed Plantings

Because of their versatility, perennials work well with lots of other kinds of plants. Try combining perennials with annuals, ornamental grasses, shrubs, or even small trees. Perennials can give structure to mixed plantings because you don't have to replace them each year.

DESIGN TIPS

The keys to successfully designing with perennials are choosing plants that do well in your growing conditions as well as choosing plants that look good both in and out of bloom. Unlike annuals, perennials aren't in bloom all season. Some may bloom for a month or more, but the average perennial is in bloom for only 1 to 2 weeks. This means the plants' foliage will be in the spotlight most of the time, so form (the overall shape of the plant) and texture (the shape of the leaves) will carry the garden through most of the season.

In addition to thinking about bloom time and foliage, you should keep color, form, and texture in mind. When you're working on your design, aim for a pleasing color scheme, but don't forget to combine foliage texture and plant shape to make your garden interesting all season. (And don't be afraid to change your design if it doesn't turn out right, even if the plants are already in the ground. After all, perennials are easy to move.)

The warm colors of yellow yarrow and red and pink astilbes pop out among the rest of your garden.

Choosing Bloom Colors

You're bound to find perennials that bloom in your favorite shades because these flowers cover the entire palette, from quiet pastels to vibrant hues of bright color. Warm colors—reds, oranges, and yellows—come forward or jump out at you. Cool colors—greens, blues,

PERENNIALS WITH FABULOUS FOLIAGE

MOST PERENNIALS BLOOM for only a few weeks, so it makes sense to think about what they'll look like the rest of the season. Here are just a few of the dual-purpose perennials available that have especially interesting (in color, shape, or both) foliage when not in flower.

Acanthus spp. (bear's breeches): Shiny; lobed or heart-shaped, spiny

Ajuga reptans (ajuga): Striking variegations and colors

Alchemilla mollis (lady's-mantle): Chartreuse; shaped like a maple leaf

Artemisia spp. (artemisias): Silver or green; aromatic; fernlike

Bergenia spp. (bergenias): Evergreen but burgundy in fall; glossy

Hosta spp. (hostas): Many solid and variegated colors; smooth or puckered surface

Polygonatum odoratum (Solomon's seal): Long, graceful shoots; green or variegated

Pulmonaria spp. (lungworts): Dark green or variegated

Sedum spp. (sedums): Many colors, variegated forms; fleshy

Stachys byzantina (lamb's-ears): Silver-gray; velvety

Yucca spp. (yuccas): Evergreen; large and sharply pointed

and purples—are softer and more subtle and have a calming effect. They retreat from the eye and seem farther away.

If your garden is far from your viewing point, choose bright colors or create more contrast. If you'll look at your garden at close range, go for a more subtle or harmonious scheme. Create the illusion of depth in a small or shallow garden by using blue and purple flowers toward the back. To add excitement, use bright colors or add a dash of red to a more subdued combination.

Considering Plant Form

You'll get the most pleasing composition if you combine flat, rounded, and spiky forms of plants. Remember to consider the shape of the leaves as well as the flowers, because the shape of the plant in full bloom may differ significantly from that the rest of the year. For example, a Siberian iris has stiff, straplike foliage and creates a vertical accent with its spiky form when not in bloom. But when the iris blooms, the masses of flat flowers give the iris plant a rounded look.

Full-grown plant height is another thing to keep in mind when thinking of overall form. Height affects the form of the garden as a whole as well as the forms of individual plants. The general rule is to place low plants at the front of the border, and work upward to tall plants as you go to the back. Of course, rules were made to be broken, which is why it's okay to add interest by putting some tall plants in the middle of the planting. (Spiky forms or vertical plants such as lilies and phlox are best for this.)

Tall plants—such as foxglove, lupines, and poppies—draw the eye to the back of the perennial border.

Perennials that have outstanding foliage, such as hostas, work well to add interest and diversity to the garden.

Selecting for Texture

Texture is also an important quality to think about when designing with perennials. You can use the rich diversity of leaf shapes and sizes to add interest to the garden when plants aren't in bloom. Team the rounded, deeply veined leaves of hostas with the straplike leaves of daylilies and the lustrous lobed leaves of peonies. Foliage also can accent other plants—for example, mounds of candytuft form an adoring base around a clump of daylilies.

TOUGH PLANTS FOR TOUGH PLACES

Every landscape has areas that offer less than ideal conditions for gardening. In fact, you may be quite familiar with sites that are too dry or too moist, or places where the sun's rays rarely shine. That doesn't mean you can't grow perennials, though. You just need to choose the plants that will thrive in your particular conditions. (On these two pages, the plant names are followed by general bloom times and colors.)

Best Perennials for Dry Soil

These perennials tolerate heat and dry soil, making them useful for spots the hose can't reach and perfect for sunny meadow gardens. All prefer well-drained soil.

Achillea **spp.** (yarrows): Late spring, summer, early fall; white, pink, red, or yellow

Artemisia **spp.** (artemisias): Summer, fall; yellowish or grayish

Coreopsis **spp.** (coreopsis): Early summer, midfall; yellow or pink

Dianthus **spp.** (pinks): Spring, summer; white, pink, or red

Euphorbia **spp.** (spurges): Spring, summer; yellow (orange and red leaves in fall)

Hemerocallis **spp.** (daylilies): Spring, summer; cream, yellow, orange, red, maroon, or pink

Rudbeckia **spp.** (coneflowers, black-eyed Susans): Summer; orange or yellow

Solidago **spp.** (goldenrods): Late summer, to fall; yellow

Stachys **spp.** (lamb's-ears, betony): Spring; purple

Best Perennials for Moist Soil

Grow these perennials if you have a poorly drained or boggy spot in your yard. Most prefer at least partial shade and cool nights.

Astilbe **spp.** (astilbes, false spireas): Late spring, summer; red, pinks, purples, cream, or white

Daylilies can add a blast of color in sites with dry soil.

***Cimicifuga* spp.** (bugbanes): Late summer, fall; white

Iris ensata (Japanese iris): Summer; pink, blue, purple, or white

Iris siberica (Siberian iris): Spring; blue, white, purple, or wine red

Lobelia siphilitica (great blue lobelia): Late summer; blue

Mertensia virginica (Virginia bluebells): Spring; blue or white

Monarda didyma (bee balm, bergamot): Summer; red, pink, white, or purple

Primula japonica (Japanese primrose): Late spring; white, pink, purple, red, or yellow

Best Perennials for Shade

Believe it or not, you have dozens of choices when it comes to perennials for shady sites. Most of these perennials prefer woodland conditions: rich, moist, well-drained soil and cool temperatures. Many plants on this list also grow well in partial shade.

***Aconitum* spp.** (monkshoods): Summer, early fall; blue

***Aquilegia* spp.** (columbines): Late spring, early summer; all colors, bicolors

***Astilbe* spp.** (astilbes, false spireas): Late spring, summer; red, pinks, purples, cream, or white

***Dicentra* spp.** (bleeding hearts): Spring, summer; pink or white

***Epimedium* spp.** (barrenworts): Spring; white, yellow, pink, or red

***Helleborus* spp.** (hellebores): Late winter, spring; pink, green, purple, red, yellow, or white

***Heuchera* spp.** (alumroots, coral bells): Spring, summer; white, pink, or red

***Hosta* spp.** (hostas, plantain lilies): Summer, fall; purple, lilac, or white

***Polygonatum* spp.** (Solomon's seals): Spring; white

***Pulmonaria* spp.** (lungworts): Spring; pink, blue, red, or white

Have poorly drained soil? Try summer-blooming bee balm, which likes moist spots.

Brighten up shady areas with hellebores—the first harbingers of spring.

SMART SHOPPING

The best perennial garden begins long before you purchase your plants. Examine your landscape, do your research, then make a list of the plants you want and stick to it. Flower shopping can be addictive, so if you don't stick to your list, you might end up with a cart full of mixed plants that caught your eye but have no place in your garden.

You can buy perennials in person (at your local garden or home center) or by mail (from catalogs or through the Internet).

In Person

Buying at a garden or home center has an advantage: You can see what you're getting before you purchase it. In fact, many garden centers have display gardens where you can see the mature sizes of the plants. The plants will be larger than those available by mail, and they'll become established more quickly. However, your selection may be limited.

When buying plants at a garden center, make sure to choose those with lush foliage.

When purchasing perennials in person, keep the following tips in mind:

- The best selection is available in spring.
- If you want a specific color, buy a named cultivar.
- Avoid plants that are obviously rootbound.
- Choose plants with lush, nicely colored foliage and multiple stems.
- Avoid plants that have insects on the tops or undersides of the leaves or along the stems.

If you're buying plants in the fall, check out the roots before you do anything else. If the roots are in good shape, then the plant is likely to be healthy—even if the plant looks kind of straggly from sitting out all summer.

By Mail

A good rule to follow when ordering perennials by mail is to start small because you can't check out the plants before you buy. So, order just a few plants at a time from several different nurseries until you find the company that delivers the quality you want.

Some nurseries ship in containers; other ship bareroot. If you live in the North, specify shipping times when ordering from southern nurseries. If you don't, your plants might arrive in spring before you're able to work the ground, or in fall after the ground has frozen.

If you decide to buy your plants by mail, remember the following points:

- Order early for the best selection.
- When ordering, specify when you want the plants to be shipped.
- Check out the roots on bareroot plants as soon as you receive them; if they're not plentiful and in good condition, return the plants immediately.
- Avoid unbeatable bargains and unbelievable claims. If it sounds too good to be true, it usually is.

quick tip

These days, you can also order plants from most nurseries through the Internet. Usually, you can get the same comprehensive information on-line that you can through their printed catalogs. When shopping on-line, follow the same tips as for shopping by mail—especially remember to specify the shipping date for your plants.

Caring for perennials involves the
basics—watering and weeding.

chapter four

Planting & Caring for Perennials

Taking the time to prepare the soil, follow general planting guidelines, weed, and control bad bugs will be well worth the effort. Your payoff? Loads of beautiful blooms that will grace your landscape for years to come.

SIZING UP YOUR SOIL

Good soil is the backbone of any good garden and is key to growing lush plants. Well-prepared soil is fluffy and loose, so water, air, and nutrients can filter down easily and plant roots have room to stretch. Most soils in residential areas are loams—combinations of sand, silt, and clay. If your soil has a high percentage of sand, it's a sandy loam, whereas if your soil has a high percentage of clay, it's a clay loam.

How do you know if you have good loam soil, or too much clay or sand? Try one of these simple tests to find out what's going on down below.

> **Well-prepared soil is the backbone of any good garden.**

The Watering Test

When you're watering plants in your garden, does the water disappear so fast it looks like only the leaves have gotten wet, rather than the soil surface? And do you find you have to water frequently to keep plants from wilting? If so, you have a lot of sand in your soil.

On the other hand, if water puddles up and seems to take forever to sink into the soil, you have lots of

When you water your garden, note what the water does to help you determine what type of soil you have.

Squeezing a handful of moist garden soil is another good way to find out if your soil has too much clay or sand.

clay. Soil with a high clay content may dry and crack apart in clods or plates between rains, and it becomes sticky or very slippery when it gets wet.

The Soil Ball Test

Try this test after a rain or after you water, when the soil is moist but not soggy. Pick up a handful of soil from the site where you want to grow perennials and squeeze it. If the soil crumbles apart when you open your hand, the soil is loam. If the soil stays in a ball, it's mostly clay. If it disintegrates easily and you can see and feel gritty little crystals in it, it's a sandy soil. And if the soil crumbles but feels greasy, it's mostly silt.

Understanding pH

Soil pH is a measure of acidity or alkalinity. It's measured on a scale from 1.0 (highly acidic) to 14.0 (highly alkaline), with 7.0 considered neutral. Most garden perennials grow best in soil with a pH of 6.0 to 7.0—slightly acidic to neutral. You can test your soil's pH yourself with a home test kit (available from garden centers and through mail-order catalogs).

Bring very acid soils closer to neutral by adding lime (often in the form of limestone); neutralize highly alkaline soils with sulfur. Adding organic matter such as leaves, grass clippings, or compost to your soil will soon bring a soil into balance—and create happier plants.

AMENDING YOUR SOIL

Soil amendments benefit your garden by supplying the material (humus) that's the basis for good plant growth. Adding amendments loosens the soil, helps the soil retain water better, and improves drainage. All garden soils, even good garden loams, benefit from regular additions of organic material. And you need to apply amendments every season because organic material is constantly being broken down in the soil.

To give your perennial plants the benefits of organic matter, you must give your soil a steady supply: Add compost and mulch to established beds, or incorporate organic material into new beds.

The most commonly available soil amendments are the following:

- Compost
- Aged manure
- Grass clippings
- Shredded leaves
- Hay and straw
- Aged sawdust

Compost and **aged manure** are balanced amendments, which means that they contain a mix of nutrients and you can add them to the soil as-is, at any time. **Grass clippings** are a good source of fast-release nitrogen, but they decompose quickly, adding little bulk to the soil. However, **shredded leaves**, **hay**, **straw**, and **aged sawdust** all need time to break down. If you want to add one of those amendments, prepare your beds in fall for spring planting or in spring for fall planting.

Don't let those fall leaves go to waste. Rake them up, shred them, and use them to amend your soil.

CREATING A NEW PERENNIAL BED

WHETHER YOU'RE DIGGING your very first perennial bed or adding another one to your landscape, the first thing you should do is test the soil moisture in the area you want to plant. Why? Because if you dig the bed when the soil is wet, you'll destroy the soil's structure and compact it; if you dig when the soil is powder dry, you'll destroy the structure and cause erosion. The best time to work the soil is when it's slightly moist.

Step 1

Step 2

Step 3

Digging a new bed isn't complicated; here's how you can do it in just five steps.

1. Mark off the area for your new bed using lime, flour, stakes and string, or a garden hose.

2. Slice off the sod in the marked area by sliding a spade under the roots. (You can add the sod to your compost pile, or use it to patch any sparse areas in your lawn.)

3. Using a garden fork, turn over all the soil in the area to be planted to the depth of the fork's tines.

4. Add compost or other organic matter and any soil amendments, then turn over the soil again with your fork to incorporate these materials and to break up clods of soil.

5. If you're going to plant in the bed immediately, water the area, let it dry, and repeat several times to help the soil settle.

Note: The soil will settle on its own if you prepare the bed in fall for spring planting or in spring for fall planting, as long as you mulch it to keep out weeds and then just let it sit until you're ready to plant.

PUTTING IN THE PLANTS

You can plant perennials any time the soil is workable, although spring and fall are best for most plants. If the plants arrive or you buy them before you're ready to plant, be sure to care for them properly until you can get them into the ground. (See "Once the Plants Come Home" on page 30 for how to do just that.) Try to plant on an overcast day, and avoid planting during midday heat.

Planting Container-Grown Perennials

Place container-grown plants on top of the soil according to your design. Start small, removing and planting one plant at a time rather than taking them all out of their pots and leaving them to dehydrate. And don't just grab a plant by the stem and pull it out of its pot. Instead, follow these simple but important steps:

1. Spread your hand over the surface of the soil with your fingers on either side of the plant stem.

2. Invert the pot so it's resting upside down on your hand, then pull off the pot with the other hand. (If the pot doesn't release easily, gently tap it a few times, and try again. If it's really stubborn, cut it off.)

If the roots have filled the pot so tightly that they hold their shape once you've removed the pot, gently pull them loose or quarter the rootball before planting.

Remove container-grown plants carefully, making sure the top of the rootball is resting securely in your hand.

ONCE THE PLANTS COME HOME

YOU MAY NOT be ready to plant when your perennials arrive in the mail or the minute you bring them home from the nursery or garden center. Although you don't have to plant right away, you can do a few things to get your perennials off to a good start before you put them in the ground.

If you receive your plants by mail, take them out of their shipping boxes immediately. Set all the plants under trees or some-place where they'll be pro-tected from full sun until you can plant them. Water container-grown plants regu-larly, and keep the material that's packed around the roots of bareroot plants damp.

Try out your container-grown perennial in the hole you've dug to make sure the hole is deep enough. But before you actually plant, remember to slice the rootball into four equal sections.

3. Hold the plant upside down, with your fingers on ei-ther side of the stem (as you removed it from the pot). Use a sharp knife or trowel to slice the rootball from the bottom up into four equal sections.

4. Spread out the four quarters in the planting hole to make sure the roots grow into the soil instead of remaining in a ball.

Plant container-grown perennials at the level at which they sat in the pots. If the crowns (where the roots meet the stems) are buried, the plants will have a tough time surviving.

Planting Bareroot Perennials

Right before you plant a bareroot perennial (they ar-rive with their roots in a protective substance, such as shredded wood, as opposed to actually being planted in a soil-filled container), cut off any dead, damaged, or diseased roots with a sharp knife. Mound soil in the bottom of the planting hole and spread the roots out so the crown of the plant rests on top of the mound. Then add soil around the roots to fill the hole.

Note: On a bareroot perennial, you'll have to determine the depth to which the plant was planted at the nursery or identify the crown. If you see a soil line or notice a spot where stems or leaf bases change color (green to yellow or green to white), plant it at that depth. If not, plant it so the soil comes up to but not past the point where the roots end and the stems begin.

CARING FOR PERENNIALS

After you've invested time, money, and energy in your perennial garden, you'll want to keep it looking its best. That's where regular (at least a few times a week) attention to watering, mulching, weeding, and grooming comes in.

Watering

When it comes to watering perennials, keep two rules in mind: Water deeply (really soaking the soil, not just sprinkling it), and water the roots (that is, on the ground around the plants, not into the air or onto the plants). If you break these rules, there's a

A soaker hose lets you give your plants evenly moist soil when Mother Nature isn't cooperating.

AFTER YOU PLANT

YOU SHOULD always keep the identification labels with perennials, no matter how many you plant. Insert identification tags (which either came with your store-bought plants or you made when you sowed the seeds) firmly into the ground at the base of the plant, where you can locate them but they'll be discreetly hidden as the plant grows. This way, if you forget what a particular plant is, you'll easily be able to find out.

Once your plants are in the ground, water them in thoroughly. Keep an eye on them over the next few weeks to make sure they don't dry out. Otherwise, leave them alone—and wait for them to start growing.

good chance you'll end up with shallow-rooted, wilt-prone plants and mildewed foliage.

With a few exceptions, perennials like consistently and evenly moist soil. In general, water when the top inch or two of soil dries out and Mother Nature isn't planning on providing any rain in the near future. Also, use a hose instead of a sprinkler so you can direct the water to the bases of the plants without wetting the foliage. For best results, don't water in the evening, when the water will stay on your plants all night, encouraging powdery mildew to grow.

Mulching

After good soil, mulch does more for plants than any technique you could use or any other product you could add to your garden. It helps maintain soil moisture (allowing you to water less often), keeps weeds at bay (giving you more time to enjoy your garden), adds nutrients to the soil (cutting down on the need to add fertilizer), and prevents erosion (see Chapter 2 for more information about mulch).

Grass clippings make excellent mulch and add nitrogen to the soil as they break down.

Apply organic mulch—shredded leaves, straw, bark, pine needles, or lawn clippings—around plants you've just planted, leaving about an inch of space around the stem of each plant. (Covering the crowns with mulch encourages crown rot.) If your mulch begins to break down and look thin as summer wears on, add more. After your plants have been killed by a hard frost in the fall, mulch fall transplants or put a winter mulch on your beds. The next spring, pull back the winter mulch until the soil has warmed, then pull it back up around your plants.

Weeding

Weeding is a fact of life for every gardener, whether you're a beginner or have been gardening for 25 years. The best way to beat these less-than-desirable plants is to start weeding as soon as you see a problem. You'll have a much harder time beating weeds if you let them take over your garden and then try to bring things under control all at once.

Even if you pull 'em as you see 'em, you'll still want to spend as little time as possible fighting weeds. Here are a few ways you can do just that.

You'll have a good shot at beating weeds if you make sure to remove them before they set seed.

- Mulch your garden. Mulch suppresses weed germination and makes the weeds that do appear easier to pull, because the soil stays soft and moist beneath the mulch.

- Remove the whole weed—roots and all—the first time. A lot of weeds can spread from a tiny piece of root or stem left in the ground.

- Don't let weeds set seed. Some perennials, such as coneflowers, self-sow so enthusiastically that they could be considered weeds. If you don't plan on starting your own nursery, cut the flower heads before the seeds ripen and drop.

- Don't compost mature weed seed heads. Although a really hot compost pile will kill weed seeds, you can't guarantee that the seeds will be in the hottest part of the pile or that your pile will get hot enough to kill all of them.

Grooming

Grooming techniques, such as thinning, pinching, and deadheading, are fast and easy techniques that will put the finishing touches on your perennial garden.

Thinning is removing some of the stems of dense, bushy plants to let in additional light and improve air circulation. This technique helps prevent mildew on susceptible plants such as garden phlox, bee balms, and delphiniums. Thin in spring by cutting or pinching out stems at the soil level. Thin each plant to the four or five strongest shoots, leaving 2 to 4 inches between each stem.

Pinching creates more compact, bushier plants, prevents flopping, and ensures more bloom. Using your forefinger and thumb, pinch out the tips of the stems. From each pinched stem, two branches will grow. Start pinching plants in late spring or early summer. Pinch again a few weeks later to encourage even bushier plants with still more flowers, but don't pinch back after flower buds are set, or you'll discourage (rather than encourage) flowering.

Despite its gory name, **deadheading,** or removing spent flowers, is a very useful technique. Some perennials deadhead themselves, dropping old flowers to

Use your forefinger and thumb to pinch out the tips of stems—pinching encourages more bloom.

the ground. But the brown, papery ruins of other flowers will spoil the beauty of your garden unless you take them off regularly. Deadheading provides your perennials with more than good looks, though. It's also important for the following reasons:

- The plant can channel energy that would normally be used to produce seed back into flower, leaf, and root production.
- Invasive perennials are kept from self-sowing all over your garden.
- The bloom season often is extended because the plants will keep flowering rather than stopping after the first bloom.

For plants that have more than one flower on a single stalk and the flowers open at different times, like daylilies, carefully snap off or pinch the faded blooms between your fingers. With plants that bear one flower head on the end of each stalk, like yarrow, cut the stalks at or near the ground when the flowers fade.

Help daylilies channel energy back into flower production by snapping off faded blooms.

quick tip

Curb the often-leggy habit of these perennials by pinching back the stems when growth takes off in the spring. You'll be rewarded with compact growth and more flowers.

Artemisia

Asters

Boltonia

Chrysanthemum

Lobelia

Monarda didyma
(wild bee balm)

Phlox

Salvia spp. (sages)

Sedum

CONTROLLING PESTS & DISEASES

The more you know about the bugs and diseases that can damage your perennials, the better off you'll be when it comes to preventing problems—and controlling them when necessary, before things get out of hand.

Pests That Affect Perennials

Control aphids the low-tech way by using a strong spray of water.

◄---- APHIDS

What they look like: Adults are tiny; pear-shaped; and green, reddish, or blue-black.

What they do: Suck plant sap, causing leaves and buds to become deformed. They also excrete honey-dew (a sticky substance) on which a black, sooty mold grows.

How you can control them: Wash them from plants with a strong spray of water; spray insecticidal soap on serious infestations.

Plants attacked: Many

If you use Japanese beetle traps, be sure to place them at least 50 feet away from your beds.

◄---- JAPANESE BEETLES

What they look like: Adults are ½-inch-long, metallic blue or metallic green beetles with pretty, coppery wing covers.

What they do: Chew on leaves and flowers, skele-tonizing foliage.

How you can control them: Handpick adults and drop them into soapy water.

Plants attacked: Asters, astilbes, *Digitalis* spp. (foxgloves), *Gaillardia* spp. (blanket flowers), *Hemerocallis* spp. (daylilies), *Paeonia* spp. (peonies)

--- LEAFMINERS --------

What they look like: Adults are ¹⁄₁₀ inch long, wasplike, and have yellow-striped black bodies with clear wings.

What they do: Disfigure foliage by creating slender, whitish, snaking tunnels as they feed.

How you can control them: Prune off and destroy infested leaves. Spray leaves weekly with insecticidal soap at the first sign of these pests. Remove garden debris in the fall.

Plants attacked: *Aquilegia* spp. (columbines), chrysanthemums, delphiniums, *Dianthus* spp. (pinks), *Heuchera* spp. (coral bells), lobelias, *Primula* spp. (primroses), salvias, verbenas

Help eliminate leafminers by pruning off infested leaves.

--- SLUGS & SNAILS --------

What they look like: Adults are ⅛ inch to 8 inches long and are gray, tan, green, black, yellow, or spotted, with eyes at the tips of small antennae. Snails have a single spiral shell; slugs do not have a shell.

What they do: Chew large holes in foliage and stems.

How you can control them: Place copper strips around your beds to prevent their entry to the garden or place small, clean dishes (the size of a cat food or tuna can) of beer around the garden to drown them. At night, handpick slugs and snails and drop into soapy water to drown them. Sprinkle sawdust around plants.

Plants attacked: *Campanula* spp. (bellflowers), delphiniums, *Hemerocallis* spp. (daylilies), hostas, irises, *Primula* spp. (primroses), sedums

Trap slimy slugs (top) and snails (bottom) by putting small dishes of beer in your beds.

Spider mites leave their mark of fine webbing over plant leaves.

SPIDER MITES

What they look like: Adults are tiny—1/50 inch long—reddish brown or pale green or yellow and have eight legs.

What they do: Cause leaves to yellow, dry up, and die. Excessive feeding turns foliage almost white; fine webs cover leaves.

How you can control them: Spray plants daily with a strong stream of water, and keep plants moist. Spray insecticidal soap sprays on serious infestations.

Plants attacked: Delphiniums, *Dianthus* spp. (pinks, carnations), *Hemerocallis* spp. (daylilies), phlox

Leave thrips homeless for the winter by keeping your garden weed-free.

THRIPS

What they look like: Adults are 1/50 to 1/25 inch long and have yellow, brown, or blackish bodies and two pairs of fringed wings.

What they do: Feed on leaves, stunting the leaves' growth. Damage may cause the tops of plants to turn brown and die.

How you can control them: Remove and destroy infested plant parts. Keep your garden weed-free because thrips overwinter in weeds. Spray insecticidal soap on serious infestations.

Plants attacked: Begonias, *Campanula* spp. (bell flowers), irises, *Paeonia* spp. (peonies)

quick tip

Help prevent the bad guys from getting a foothold in your plants by giving them a snack of compost tea. Simply soak a cloth bag full of finished compost in a watering can or barrel for several days. Then use the tea to water your plants—or put it in a spray bottle and spray it on plant leaves.

Diseases That Affect Perennials

--- BACTERIAL LEAF SPOT ---

Cause: Bacterial infection

Symptoms: Many small brown or purple spots on plant leaves; heavily spotted leaves may yellow and drop.

Controls: Remove and destroy infected plants, and wash your hands (with soap and water) and tools (with a solution of one part bleach to nine parts water) after handling diseased plants. Avoid splashing water on plant foliage.

Always wash your tools after working on plants with bacterial leaf spot.

Plants affected: Delphiniums, *Geranium* spp. (cranesbills), *Hemerocallis* spp. (daylilies), irises, *Paeonia* spp. (peonies), *Prunella* spp. (self-heal)

--- DOWNY MILDEW ---

Cause: Fungal infection

Symptoms: Cottony gray or white spots on the undersides of leaves; angular yellow spots on the tops of leaves.

Controls: Grow resistant varieties. Space plants to encourage air circulation between them, and avoid wetting the foliage when watering. Clean up garden debris in the fall.

Water plants as close to the soil as possible to avoid wetting their leaves and encouraging downy mildew.

Plants affected: Arabis (rock cress), artemisias, asters, *Geranium* spp. (hardy geraniums), *Lupinus* spp. (lupines), *Rudbeckia* spp. (black-eyed Susans), *Veronica* spp. (speedwells)

Give your plants breathing room to help prevent powdery mildew.

POWDERY MILDEW

Cause: Fungal infection

Symptoms: White powdery spots on leaves that enlarge quickly, covering the entire leaf, flower, or shoot. Leaves may drop off.

Controls: Grow resistant varieties. Space plants to encourage air circulation between them. Remove and destroy infected leaves. Water in the morning, and avoid wetting the foliage.

Plants affected: *Achillea* spp. (yarrows), asters, coreopsis, delphiniums, *Echinacea* spp. (purple coneflowers), *Erigeron* spp. (fleabanes), *Lupinus* spp. (lupines), *Monarda* spp. (bee balms, bergamots), phlox, *Pulmonaria* spp. (lungworts), *Rudbeckia* spp. (coneflowers, black-eyed Susans), *Solidago* spp. (goldenrods)

Well-drained soil is key to avoiding root rot.

ROOT ROT

Cause: Poorly drained soil

Symptoms: Yellow leaves, slow plant growth, the roots rot off (causing the plant to topple at the crown).

Controls: Plant perennials in well-drained soil; avoid damaging roots when digging around plants; keep mulch away from the base of plants. Wash tools between plants. Remove and destroy infected plants.

Plants affected: Many, including *Artemisia* spp. (wormwood) and *Cerastium* spp. (snow-in-summer)

--- RUST ---

Cause: Fungal infection

Symptoms: Powdery orange spots on the undersides of leaves

Controls: Grow resistant varieties; keep leaves dry; thin stems to encourage air circulation. Remove and destroy infected plant parts.

Plants affected: *Achillea* spp. (yarrows), *Aquilegia* spp. (columbines), *Campanula* spp. (bellflowers), delphiniums, *Dianthus* spp. (pinks, carnations), irises, *Liatris* spp. (gayfeathers), *Monarda* spp. (bee balms, bergamots)

Those powdery orange spots are a dead giveaway for rust.

--- WILT ---

Cause: Fungal infection

Symptoms: Infected leaves and stems wilt; leaves may yellow and curl upward, then drop off.

Controls: Dig up and destroy infected plants. Clean up garden debris well in the fall. Plant resistant varieties.

Plants affected: Chrysanthemums, *Dianthus* spp. (pinks, carnations), asters, coreopsis, delphiniums, *Paeonia* spp (peonies), *Papaver* spp. (poppies), phlox

You can help get rid of wilt by digging up and destroying infected plants.

HOT STUFF

IF A SOILBORNE problem like wilt has plagued your perennials for seasons at a time, you might be able to give it the heave-ho with soil solarization. Although this is an easy technique, you have to start with a new bed.

In spring in the South and in midsummer in the North, rake the new bed smooth and water it well. Dig a trench several inches deep around the outside of the bed. Spread a thin, clear plastic sheet over the bed and press it down against the soil surface. Press the edges of the sheet into the trench, and seal the plastic by filling the trench with soil. Leave the sheet in place for 1 to 2 months.

This technique works because heat builds up under the plastic sheet, essentially cooking the top 6 to 12 inches of soil—and any diseases in it.

PREDICTING WHICH plants will be the favorites for the deer population in your neighborhood is impossible. But some gardeners have reported success with the list below. Use it as your starting point, then experiment to find out which perennials don't appeal to deer in your area.

Aquilegia spp. (columbines)

Astilbes

Dicentra spectabilis (common bleeding heart)

Digitalis spp. (foxgloves)

Gaillardia spp. (blanket flowers)

Geranium spp. (cranesbills)

Helleborus spp. (hellebores)

Hemerocallis spp. (daylilies)

Irises

Liatris spp. (gayfeathers)

Monarda didyma (bee balm)

Pulmonaria spp. (lungworts)

Salvias

MANAGING ANIMAL PESTS

Unless you garden in a cage, animal pests—including a neighborhood cat—are bound to pay your perennials a visit. A few strategies can help you deter local wild and domestic animals safely and humanely, without losing your perennials in the process.

Discouraging Deer

Deer are determined creatures when it comes to snacking. They effortlessly jump 4-foot fences and will happily snack on just about any of your plants that they can reach. Short of spending lots of money on fencing, you may have success with the following techniques:

Deodorize 'em. Buy several bars of the smelliest brand of deodorant soap you can find. Drill one hole through each bar (wrapper and all), insert a piece of wire (10 to 12 inches ought to be enough) through the hole, and twist the wire to secure the soap. Hang bars about 3 feet off the ground all around your garden.

Whip 'em up. Break a few egg yolks into a bowl, whip them with a whisk or a fork, mix them with a gallon of water, and spray your plants generously. Repeat as necessary, especially after rainfall.

Stink bomb 'em. Here's a new use for smelly old sweatsocks and t-shirts, if you can stand it: Discreetly hang them around the perimeter of your garden. (Don't wash them after wearing, or you'll remove the odor!) Cloth bags of hair clippings also help repel deer.

Fake 'em out. Although deer will eat just about anything if they're hungry, some plants simply don't taste good to them. See "Perennials That Deter Deer" on this page for a list of perennials that deer are less likely to munch.

Repelling Rabbits

Sure, bunnies are cute—until they nibble your perennials to the ground. Rabbits tend to pose problems primarily in early spring, when tender new shoots sprout up, and in winter, when food is scarce.

To foil bunnies in spring, try spreading the thorny clippings from your roses or brambles around the plants that rabbits favor. If the rabbit damage is severe, you may need to use low fencing around your perennial beds for season-long protection.

To prevent winter nibbling, cover tasty plants with wire mesh cages in fall; remove the cages in spring after plants are well established.

Thwart Peter Rabbit by spreading thorny clippings around his favorite plants.

FOILING FIDO AND FLUFFY

ALTHOUGH DOGS AND CATS can be your best friends, they can also be your worst enemies when it comes to wreaking havoc on your garden. Dogs love to dig in garden beds to bury their treasures, and cats love to get their paws in the dirt because it makes a perfect litter box. Here are some defensive tactics for keeping these four-legged friends out of your perennial beds.

Dogs

- Install temporary fencing to protect new plants until they're established.

- If possible, put up a low fence around your entire property to thwart neighborhood dogs.

- Arrange your garden with mulched or mown paths so your dog has a place to run without trampling your plants.

Cats

- Cover new beds or plantings with wire mesh, chicken wire, or hardware fabric. Cats' sensitive paws won't like the feeling as they scratch, so they'll move on.

- Scatter thorny or prickly clippings from roses or brambles on your beds; just be careful not hurt yourself when you work in the garden.

When it comes to choosing and using perennials, you don't have to follow anyone's rules but your own.

chapter five

Perennial Favorites

With so many beautiful, dependable perennials to choose from, deciding which ones to plant in your garden can be tough. In this chapter, you'll learn about 50 outstanding plants—perennials that have been loved by gardeners for years and are just waiting to grace your flowerbeds.

CHOOSE CAREFULLY

Once you start flipping through the following pages, you'll probably want to plant at least one of each kind of perennial listed here. But hold on a minute before you rush gung ho to your local garden center. Take the time to read the "Plant Particulars" listed for each entry—especially the appropriate USDA Plant Hardiness Zones (see page 106 if you don't know your zone) for each perennial that interests you. Then, consider the available light as well as the soil characteristics in each area of your yard that you want to plant. The perennials you choose should be those best suited to growth in your region and under the conditions specific to your landscape.

Plant shape, spread, height, color, and bloom time also are important factors to consider when choosing perennials. If you have limited room, rule out plants that spread aggressively, or they'll quickly invade the rest of your space. Also, make sure that the shapes, heights, and colors of your chosen plants work with the overall design you have in mind.

EXPRESS YOURSELF

Now go ahead—turn the page and start dreaming about the art you'll create in your garden. Remember, anyone can create a masterpiece with perennials!

Take the time to choose perennials that are best suited to your landscape conditions.

ACHILLEA
(Yarrow)

Achillea × 'Moonshine'

PLANT PARTICULARS

Zones: 3 to 9

Height: 1 to 4 feet

Spread: Strong spreaders; depending on species, can spread between 1 and 5 feet

Shape: Spreading clumps of stiff, upright flowerstalks

Color: White, pink, red, or yellow flowers; green or gray leaves

Bloom time: Late spring or summer to early fall

Light needs: Full sun to partial shade

Soil: Average to poor; dry but well drained

YARROWS ARE THE perfect perennials to add some spice to your garden—literally—because their foliage has a spicy aroma. In addition to smelling good, yarrows are also attractive. Their showy, flattened flower heads are made up of many tiny, tightly packed flowers and their leaves are feathery. These extremely versatile plants work well in formal or informal borders and soften bold textures. Definitely plant yarrows along a walkway, where you'll be sure to brush against them, releasing their fragrance.

These low-maintenance plants thrive with little care. However, they do spread rapidly, so divide your plants every 3 to 5 years. In early spring or fall, dig up a clump, remove any dead stems from its center, break up the clump, and relocate the new plants.

Yarrows are excellent for cutting and for use in fresh and dried flower arrangements. To enjoy the flowers after the growing season has ended, cut the blooms before their color starts to fade; tie the stems in bunches; and hang them upside down in a dark, airy room (such as an attic) until dry. ❋

ALCHEMILLA
(Lady's-Mantle)

Alchemilla vulgaris

THE LEAVES OF lady's-mantle have an interesting feature: downy hairs. When water beads up on the leaves, the effect is an enchanting, jeweled display that's hard to beat. The plant also will reward you with clouds of lovely flowers and lush clumps of soft, fan-shaped foliage. This perennial works well at the front of the perennial border, along a wall, or edging a walk. Try pairing it with upright perennials, such as Siberian iris and astilbes. The small variety of lady's-mantle (*A. alpina*) is perfect for rock gardens and containers.

By midsummer, the leaves of lady's-mantle can look rather tired. To perk up the plant and encourage new foliage growth, cut it back to the ground. (The plants will quickly produce a new set of leaves.) If you live in a region where the temperature really climbs during the summer, choose a partially shaded site for best growth and flowering.

Lady's-mantle will often self-sow; cut off spent flowers to prevent reseeding. Relocate new seedlings to extend an edging all along a bed. Divide overgrown clumps in spring or fall. ❖

PLANT PARTICULARS

Zones: 3 to 8

Height: 6 to 12 inches

Spread: 1 to 2 feet

Shape: Soft mounds

Color: Chartreuse flowers; gray-green leaves

Bloom time: Spring, early summer

Light needs: Sun to partial shade

Soil: Rich; moist

ANEMONE
(Anemone, Windflower)

Anemone × hybrida (Japanese anemone)

PLANT PARTICULARS

Zones: 3 to 9

Height: 4 inches to 5 feet

Spread: 18 to 24 inches

Shape: Varies among species

Color: White, pink, red, purple, or blue flowers with yellow centers; deep green foliage

Bloom time: Spring, summer, fall

Light needs: Full sun to partial shade

Soil: Fertile but well drained

ONE OF THE great things about anemones is that they come in spring-, summer-, and fall-blooming varieties—which means you can have a full season of anemone color. Anemones have fragile, five-petaled flowers with fuzzy, bright yellow centers. These perennials can work well as mass plantings, in combination with spring bulbs, under shrubs, or as a groundcover, depending on the variety.

If you have room for only one anemone, make it a Japanese anemone (*Anemone × hybrida*). This fall-blooming beauty has single or double flowers on 3- to 5-foot stems. Combine Japanese anemones with bleeding hearts and other early bloomers; the anemone foliage will fill the space when the other plants go dormant.

To increase your anemone collection, divide spring-blooming types after flowering and summer and fall bloomers in spring.

Note: All anemones are poisonous if eaten, so you might want to avoid planting them if small children frequently visit your garden. ✳

Hybrid columbines

IF YOU WANT to attract hummingbirds to your garden, then add columbine to your beds. Each blossom has five petals, which form a tube that holds the nectar that hummingbirds desire. These delicate-looking perennials come in shades of blue, maroon, pink, purple, red, white, or yellow that add charm to borders, woodland gardens, and rock gardens and also bridge the spring and summer bloom seasons. Combine them with late-blooming tulips to finish the spring show, and with irises and peonies to start your summer display. They also look super around the base of tall, shrubby perennials, such as baptisias and delphiniums.

In mid- to late summer, the urn-shaped seedpods will drop lots of seed and self-sow. To prevent self-sowing, pinch off spent flowers. Otherwise, relocate the seedlings in spring.

Squiggly lines on your columbine leaves indicate that leafminers are at work. Immediately pinch off and destroy the damaged leaves, and check the plants frequently for more signs of damage. If the problem is severe, spray the plants weekly with insecticidal soap. ✻

PLANT PARTICULARS

Zones: 3 to 9

Height: 6 inches to 4 feet

Spread: 1 foot

Shape: Open clumps

Color: Blue, maroon, pink, purple, red, white, or yellow flowers; blue-green to green leaves

Bloom time: Late spring to early summer

Light needs: Full sun to partial shade

Soil: Average to rich; moist but well drained

ARTEMISIA
(Artemisia, Wormwood)

Artemisia schmidtiana 'Silver Mound'

PLANT PARTICULARS

Zones: 3 to 9

Height: 10 inches to 6 feet

Spread: Strong spreaders; depending on species, can spread between 6 and 30 inches

Shape: Varies among species

Color: Yellowish or grayish flowers; green to silver leaves

Bloom time: Summer, fall

Light needs: Full sun

Soil: Average; dry but well drained

THESE AROMATIC PLANTS are indispensable for adding year-round foliage interest to beds and borders. Artemisias have showy green or gray foliage and yellowish or grayish flowers, which appear late in the season. Some varieties form shrubby, mounding clumps, whereas others form upright, spreading clumps. Plant artemisias to contrast with bright colors in your garden (especially hot pinks, reds, and oranges) or to cool pastels (such as soft pinks, purples, and blues.)

If you prefer low-maintenance plants, then artemisias are the perennials for you. And once established, most of them are extremely drought-tolerant. If you live in a warm, humid region, plant upright varieties instead of the mounding ones, because the mounding varieties tend to fall open from the center. All artemisia varieties should be pruned back hard if they start to lose their form. ▨

Aster amellus 'King George'

BUSHY AND BEAUTIFUL, asters offer masses of showy, daisylike blooms that are ideal for edgings, containers, meadow and woodland gardens, and at the backs of beds and borders. Although you might think of asters as being primarily fall plants, many varieties begin blooming in late summer—and they come in a rainbow of colors. To create layers of texture and color, try backing pink asters with Russian sage and yellow coneflowers. Asters also pair well with ferns and wildflowers.

Tall asters probably will need staking. You also can cut them back by half in midsummer to promote sturdier stems and more branching. For bushier fall plants, pinch or shear asters in the spring or early summer. Divide plants every year or two to control their spread, rejuvenate overgrown clumps, or increase your plantings. To avoid powdery mildew, avoid wetting the leaves when watering. ❈

PLANT PARTICULARS

Zones: 2 to 8

Height: 6 inches to 8 feet

Spread: Varies among species

Shape: Varies among species

Color: Blue, purple, red, pink, or white flowers; green leaves

Bloom time: Late summer to late fall

Light needs: Full sun to light shade

Soil: Average; moist but well drained

ASTILBE
(Astilbe, False Spirea)

Astilbe × *arendsii* 'Weiss Gloria'

PLANT PARTICULARS

Zones: 3 to 9

Height: 8 inches to 5 feet

Spread: 1 to 3 feet

Shape: Clumps of upright or cascading flowerstalks

Color: Red, magenta, rose, pink, lavender, lilac, cream, or white flowers; leaves are green or reddish

Bloom time: Late spring, summer

Light needs: Full sun to deep shade

Soil: Average; moist but well drained

IF YOU'RE LOOKING for a way to add some color to a moist, shady area of your yard, then astilbes are the perennial for you. These regal plants have airy plumes of densely packed, tiny flowers that range in color from red through all shades of magenta, rose, and pink to lavender, lilac, cream, and white. The shape of the flower clusters differs by variety; some are stiff and upright, others are open plumes, and still others cascade outward like fireworks. Astilbe leaves are fernlike and have a coppery or reddish sheen in spring.

These long-lived, low-maintenance plants are perfect companions to ferns, irises, and other moisture-loving plants. You might want to try a mass of astilbes around a water garden, where the water will reflect the flower's colorful blooms.

During the summer, snip a few of the flowers to enjoy in arrangements indoors; leave the rest to mature on the plants for winter interest. ❋

BAPTISIA
(Baptisia, False Indigo)

Baptisia australis (blue false indigo)

PLANT THEM AND forget them—that's the key to growing baptisias. These durable plants can live in the same spot for years without division, slowly forming shrublike clumps. Baptisias have colorful spikes of pealike flowers in blue, yellow, cream, and white with gray-green or bluish leaves. They're excellent border plants; use them toward the back of the border in the company of bold flowers such as peonies, oriental poppies, and irises. After flowering, baptisias make a good background for late-blooming perennials. Baptisias also produce showy gray or brown seedpods; cut them for arrangements or leave them on the plants for off-season interest.

Have patience when growing baptisias; they grow slowly at first and may require at least 5 years to reach their full growth. In some spots, baptisias may need staking; place rounded peony hoops over the clumps as they emerge in early spring to keep the plants from toppling over. ❈

PLANT PARTICULARS

Zones: 3 to 9

Height: 1 to 5 feet

Spread: 3 to 4 feet

Shape: Clumps of upright flowerstalks

Color: Blue, yellow, cream, or white flowers; gray-green or bluish leaves

Bloom time: Late spring to early summer

Light needs: Full sun to partial shade

Soil: Rich; moist but well drained

BOLTONIA
(Boltonia)

Boltonia asteroides 'Pink Beauty'

PLANT PARTICULARS

Zones: 3 to 9

Height: 4 to 6 feet

Spread: 3 to 4 feet

Shape: Tall, rounded

Color: Pink, purple, or white flowers with yellow centers; blue-green leaves

Bloom time: Late spring to midfall

Light needs: Full sun to light shade

Soil: Rich; moist or dry

ADD A COOL touch to late summer and early fall borders and wildflower gardens with boltonia. This elegant perennial has blue-green leaves and purple, pale pink, or snowy white flowers with yellow centers. It's easy to grow, and it will deliver blooms in poor, dry soil as well as rich, moist soil. (Just keep in mind that the plant will be smaller in dry soil than it would be in moist soil.) For an elegant, all-white combination, try 'Snowbank' boltonia with a white-variegated ornamental grass and a white-flowered Japanese anemone.

Cut back boltonias by half in early to midsummer to encourage bushiness and flowering. You can leave the stems standing after they've finished blooming to add interest and texture to your winter garden. If you want more boltonia plants, divide them in spring. Remove the dead centers and replant the vigorous outer portions. ❉

CAMPANULA
(Bellflower)

Campanula latifolia 'Alba'

THESE EASY-CARE perennials have bell- or star-shaped flowers. They come in many different varieties, which range from low, mat-forming creepers to tall, upright plants. Choose the low-growing varieties for rock gardens and informal rock walls. The blue and purple flowers contrast well with rocks and will soften even the harshest rock surface. Use the taller varieties in beds and borders, or along walls and fences. They're also lovely in large drifts. Create stunning color combinations by grouping blue bellflowers with bright yellow yarrow, pure white peonies, and/or pretty pink astilbes.

Divide bellflowers in early spring or fall to control their spread or rejuvenate crowded clumps. Slugs are the only serious threats to bellflowers; use a dish of beer as bait to drown these pests (see "Pests That Affect Perennials" on page 36 to learn more about pest prevention and control). �

PLANT PARTICULARS

Zones: 2 to 8

Height: 4 inches to 5 feet

Spread: Varies among species

Shape: Varies among species

Color: Purple, blue, white, or pink flowers; green leaves

Bloom time: Spring, summer

Light needs: Full sun to partial shade

Soil: Average to rich; well drained

CHRYSANTHEMUM
(Chrysanthemum)

Chrysanthemum frutescens (marguerite daisy)

PLANT PARTICULARS

Zones: 3 to 11

Height: 1 to 5 feet

Spread: Varies among species

Shape: Varies among species

Color: White, yellow, orange, red, pink, or purple; leaves various shades of green

Bloom time: Summer to fall

Light needs: Full sun

Soil: Average to rich; well drained

WITH SO MANY different varieties of this perennial, you could have some sort of chrysanthemum (often shortened to "mum") blooming in your garden from early summer 'til frost. The daisylike flowers are available in shades of white, yellow, orange, red, pink, or purple. Shasta daisies and garden (hardy) mums are both types of chrysanthemums.

Mums are so varied in bloom time, color, size, and adaptability that they have a place in almost every garden. Shasta daisies, for example, are classics for the early summer garden. These white blooms create quite a pretty sight when paired with Siberian irises. And what would fall be without bright garden mums? They're perfect for tucking into bare spots in the garden left by worn-out annuals or for grouping in containers when most plants have stopped blooming for the season. Other mums work well as edging plants and at the back of beds or borders. ▨

Coreopsis 'Sterntaler'

CHEERFUL COREOPSIS IS a dependable, easy-care plant that will bloom for months as long as you remove the spent flowers. The daisylike blooms are a welcoming sight in summer beds and borders. Coreopsis combines well with asters, irises, blanket flowers, purple coneflowers, and phlox. 'Moonbeam' (*C. verticillata*) is a particularly outstanding variety; its light yellow flowers look beautiful paired with other soft colors, such as pink, blue, and lavender. For brighter yellow blooms, look for 'Zagreb'.

Coreopsis is an especially good choice for beginning gardeners. The plants grow rapidly from seed and, once established, are quite drought-tolerant and even thrive under stress. However, they do need well-drained soil and may rot if planted in a location where water puddles. They may also flop over in soil that's too rich. Divide overgrown or declining plants in spring or fall. ✽

PLANT PARTICULARS

Zones: 3 to 9

Height: 1 to 9 feet

Spread: Varies among species

Shape: Varies among species

Color: Yellow or pink flowers; green leaves

Bloom time: Early summer to midfall

Light needs: Full sun

Soil: Average to poor; dry but well drained

DELPHINIUM
(Delphinium, Larkspur)

Delphinium elatum (candle larkspur)

PLANT PARTICULARS

Zones: 3 to 8

Height: 1 to 6 feet

Spread: Varies among species

Shape: Varies among species

Color: Blue, purple, pink, or white flowers; green leaves

Bloom time: Late spring, summer; fall rebloom

Light needs: Full sun

Soil: Rich; moist but well drained

THESE TALL, STURDY, old-fashioned perennials are perfect for adding vertical accents to your garden. Their towers of showy flowers are traditional favorites for early summer color in beds, borders, and cottage gardens. Try placing them at the rear of a border, where their spikes can be highlighted against a wall or hedge. Create eye-catching contrasts by pairing delphiniums with bushy, mounded perennials such as peonies and baby's breath. To accent a wall or a fence, plant bold masses of mixed colors.

Encourage plants to rebloom by cutting off the spent flowers just above the top leaves. When the leafy stems begin to die back, cut them down to the new growth at the base of the plant.

Delphiniums are short-lived perennials, which means they fade out after 2 or 3 years in the garden. To propagate them, sow seeds outdoors in late summer; the seeds will grow and bloom the following season. ▨

DIANTHUS
(Pinks, Carnation)

Dianthus deltoides (maiden pinks)

PINKS ARE BELOVED for their old-fashioned charm and delightful spicy-sweet fragrance. Their delicate flowers have fringed petals that complement their slender leaves. What's more, the foliage holds its color year-round, making this perennial attractive even when it's not blooming.

Most varieties of pinks are low-growing, clump-forming plants that are perfect additions to rock gardens and border edgings, and great for use as ground covers. Plant them on top of a retaining wall so you won't have to kneel down to enjoy their scent. Silvery-leaved plants, such as lamb's-ears and artemisias, make striking companions for pinks' bright blooms.

Pinks spread quickly and are often short-lived, so divide the clumps every 2 or 3 years to keep the plants vigorous. If you remove the spent flowers regularly, you'll usually be able to keep your pinks in bloom for 6 weeks or more. ▨

PLANT PARTICULARS

Zones: 3 to 9

Height: 3 inches to 2 feet

Spread: 8 to 18 inches

Shape: Mounds or mats

Color: White, pink, or red flowers; blue-green leaves

Bloom time: Spring, summer

Light needs: Full sun to light shade

Soil: Average; moist to dry

DICENTRA
(Bleeding Heart)

Dicentra spectabilis 'Alba'

PLANT PARTICULARS

Zones: 2 to 9

Height: 8 inches to 2½ feet

Spread: Varies by species

Shape: Soft mounds

Color: Pink or white flowers; green to blue-green leaves

Bloom time: Spring, summer

Light needs: Full sun to full shade

Soil: Rich; moist but well drained

THE UNIQUE FLOWERS of this perennial, which resemble pink or white hearts with drops of blood on their tips, add splashes of color to any shade or woodland garden. Its feathery, fernlike foliage is a nice contrast to the plant's blooms. Some varieties are tall (common bleeding heart, *D. spectabilis*) and bloom in the spring, whereas others (fringed bleeding heart, *D. eximia*) are much smaller and bloom in summer.

Because common bleeding heart often goes dormant by midsummer, pair it with bushy plants, such as asters and baby's breath, that will fill the space it leaves. Common bleeding heart also works well with daffodils, tulips, peonies, irises, and primroses. For a steady display of flowers from spring until frost, plant fringed bleeding heart with ferns, wildflowers, and shade-loving hostas.

Divide overgrown clumps of bleeding hearts in the fall or as they go dormant. The plants often self-sow; either remove spent flowers to prevent self-sowing or transplant the seedlings. ✳

Digitalis grandiflora

HERE'S A PLANT that deer seem to avoid. These stout perennials have leafy stems and tall spikes of funnel-like flowers in shades of pink, rose, white, and yellow. The insides of the plants are often spotted. Most foxgloves are either biennials (they live 2 years) or short-lived perennials (they live about 3 years).

These striking blooms perfectly punctuate the summer border, and their upright form is a welcome contrast to mounded plants such as hostas and peonies. They also look super with ferns and hostas in shade and woodland plantings. For compact, easy-care color, try perennial yellow foxglove (*D. grandiflora*). Its 2- to 3-foot spikes of soft yellow flowers combine beautifully with blues, pinks, and whites.

Common foxglove (*D. purpurea*) reaches 5 feet high when in bloom. Although it's a biennial, common foxglove acts like a perennial because it produces lots of self-sown seedlings. You can also lift the clumps after flowering, remove the bloom stalks that are spent, and replant the new rosettes in the same spot or somewhere new. ❀

PLANT PARTICULARS

Zones: 3 to 8

Height: 2 to 5 feet

Spread: 1 to 2 feet

Shape: Erect flower spikes

Color: Pink, rose, white, or yellow flowers; green leaves

Bloom time: Summer

Light needs: Full sun to partial shade

Soil: Rich; moist but well drained

ECHINACEA
(Purple Coneflower)

Echinacea purpurea

PLANT PARTICULARS

Zones: 2 to 8

Height: 1 to 6 feet

Spread: Varies by species

Shape: Loose clumps of erect stalks

Color: Purple, pink, or white flowers; green leaves

Bloom time: Summer

Light needs: Full sun to light shade

Soil: Average; moist to dry

BUTTERFLIES LOVE TO visit purple coneflower during the blooming season, and seed-eating birds are attracted to its seedheads long after the blooms are gone. This showy perennial with daisylike flowers is also extremely heat- and drought-tolerant because the plant's thick, deep taproots store moisture in lean times. What's more, purple coneflower is about the easiest perennial to care for.

This plant is a natural choice for meadow gardens, along with ornamental grasses, goldenrods, and yarrows. In beds and borders, try pairing the bright blooms with artemisias, daylilies, coreopsis, and lamb's-ears. For a colorful late-summer display, pair purple coneflowers with black-eyed Susans.

You'll rarely need to divide purple coneflowers. (In fact, once divided, plants tend to become bushy and produce fewer flowers.) If you leave the seedheads on for winter interest, plants may self-sow. ✺

Epimedium × rubrum

THESE TOUGH PERENNIALS, once established, will perform admirably in dry shade or under mature trees where nothing else will grow. Most people grow epimediums as groundcovers. However, they also work well in beds, borders, and rock gardens—even in a shade garden with astilbes, hostas, primroses, wildflowers, bulbs, and ferns.

Their heart-shaped green leaves often have red highlights; their flowers bloom in early spring before the new leaves open. Although they're often touted as evergreens, epimediums tend to look tattered by midwinter. Cut them to the ground in early spring; the plants will look neater and the dainty flowers will be more visible. New leaves will emerge with or just after the flowers.

Epimediums form spreading clumps that seldom need division. But, if you want to divide your plants, do so in late summer or early fall. ✽

PLANT PARTICULARS

Zones: 3 to 8

Height: 6 to 15 inches

Spread: Varies by species

Shape: Spreading mats

Color: White, yellow, pink, or red flowers; green, yellow, or reddish leaves

Bloom time: Spring

Light needs: Partial to full shade

Soil: Average to rich; moist to dry

EUPHORBIA
(Spurge, Euphorbia)

Euphorbia epithymoides (cushion spurge)

PLANT PARTICULARS

Zones: 3 to 9

Height: 6 inches to 4 feet

Spread: Varies by species

Shape: Spreading clumps

Color: Yellow flowers; green or blue-green leaves

Bloom time: Spring, summer

Light needs: Full sun to partial shade

Soil: Average to rich; dry but well drained

IF YOU WANT an outstanding foliage perennial, then euphorbia is for you. Euphorbias are succulent perennials with leafy stems and milky sap that flows freely when the leaves or stems are picked or damaged. (This sap is irritating to skin, so wear gloves while working around these plants.) Combine them with other perennials or flowering shrubs at the rear of a bed or border, or use them as container plants, as a groundcover, or in a rock garden.

Cushion spurge (*E. epithymoides*) is one of the most popular species. It forms a mound of bright yellow flowers in early spring, and the leaves turn red and orange in fall. Combine its green leaves and glowing yellow petal-like bracts with brightly colored tulips for a spectacular spring display.

Euphorbias are long-lived perennials that require little care. If you live in a zone where winters are cold but you don't get a lot of snow, provide winter protection (mulch or plant covers) to prevent leaf burn and stem damage. Divide plants in spring to rejuvenate old clumps or fill out plantings. ❋

GAILLARDIA
(Blanket Flower)

Gaillardia 'Goblin'

THESE SALT- AND drought-tolerant perennials are perfect for seaside gardens and seem to thrive on neglect and heat. (Surprisingly, the only place they don't grow well is in rich, moist soil, which makes them floppy and shortens their life expectancy.) Blanket flowers produce mounds of showy daisylike flowers from early summer through fall. Plant them with other warm-colored perennials such as coreopsis, butterfly weeds, and yarrows for a harmonious display. Add interest and excitement to blanket flowers by teaming them with the spiky yellow leaves of Spanish bayonet and with purple flowers, such as sage. Gaillardia is also a great cutting flower, so make sure to add some to fresh bouquets.

Pinch off spent flowers at the tip of the stem to keep plants looking tidy and to prolong the bloom season. Blanket flowers tend to be short-lived, so divide them every 2 or 3 years in early spring to keep the clumps thriving. Sow seeds outdoors in fall or sow them indoors in winter. Seedlings may bloom the first year. 🌸

PLANT PARTICULARS

Zones: 2 to 10

Height: 2 to 3 feet

Spread: Varies by species

Shape: Spreading clumps

Color: Yellow, orange, red, and brown flowers; green or blue-green leaves

Bloom time: Spring, summer

Light needs: Full sun to partial shade

Soil: Average to rich; well drained

GERANIUM
(Cranesbill, Hardy Geranium)

Geranium 'Johnson's Blue'

PLANT PARTICULARS

Zones: 3 to 8

Height: 4 inches to 3 feet

Spread: Varies by species

Shape: Soft mounds

Color: White, blue, purple, rose, or pink flowers; green leaves that turn burgundy-red, scarlet, or orange in the fall

Bloom time: Spring, early summer

Light needs: Full sun to partial shade

Soil: Rich; moist but well drained

CRANESBILLS WILL GIVE you a long season of interest in the garden, thanks to their attractive foliage that turns colors in the fall. These geraniums have small, pretty flowers in shades of purple, rose, pink, white, or blue; the plants come in an array of heights that can fit into any planting scheme. (Don't confuse cranesbills with the tender bedding geraniums that you'll find at your local garden center—those geraniums won't survive a frost.)

A summer border wouldn't be complete without cranesbills. Combine them with bold colors and spiky forms or use them as "weavers" to tie together different combinations. Siberian iris, garden phlox, bellflowers, evening primroses, and ornamental grasses are all good companions.

It's nearly impossible to have too many of these versatile, easy-to-grow perennials, so divide and transplant existing plants in fall or early spring. Many cranesbills will also self-sow. If you catch the seeds before they're catapulted toward the neighbor's yard, sow them outdoors. ✸

HELLEBORUS
(Hellebore, Lenten Rose)

Helleborus × orientalis

THIS PERENNIAL IS what you want to plant for winter and early spring bloom and lasting foliage interest. Some hellebores have noticeable stems, and others have leaves and flowers that seem to rise directly from the ground. Their flowers come in shades of green, pink, purple, red, yellow, and white, and their leathery foliage is attractive throughout the summer, long after the blooms have faded.

Try combining hellebores with flowering shrubs that have attractive bark and early flowers; red- and yellow-stemmed dogwoods, serviceberries, and purple-leaved shrubs are good choices. The smaller bulbs, such as early crocus, reticulated iris, and species forms of daffodils and tulips are also good companions. The mottled, heart-shaped foliage of spring- or fall-blooming hardy cyclamen combines nicely with the dark green of the hellebore leaves. (Take care not to plant large floppy perennials near hellebores, which may smother the hellebores and block out the sun.)

Hellebores tend to self-sow where they are happy; transplant seedlings to other parts of the garden. ✺

PLANT PARTICULARS

Zones: 3 to 9

Height: 10 inches to 2 feet

Spread: 10 to 18 inches

Shape: Clumps of flowerstalks

Color: Green, pink, purple, red, yellow, or white flowers; dark green leaves

Bloom time: Late winter to spring

Light needs: Partial shade

Soil: Rich; moist but well drained

HEMEROCALLIS
(Daylily)

Hemerocallis 'Jake Russell'

PLANT PARTICULARS

Zones: 2 to 9

Height: 1 to 6 feet

Spread: 1 to 5 feet

Shape: Mounds of arching leaves with clumping flower-stalks

Color: Cream, yellow, orange, red, maroon, or pink flowers; green leaves

Bloom time: Spring, summer

Light needs: Full sun to partial shade

Soil: Average to rich; dry but well drained

TOUGH, ADAPTABLE DAYLILIES are easy to grow. These popular perennials have colorful flowers that each last only a day—but a profusion of new buds keeps plants in bloom for 2 to 4 weeks.

Daylilies make great companion plants for spring bulbs, such as daffodils. The bulbs bloom as the daylily leaves emerge; then, the daylily foliage takes over as the bulb leaves turn yellow in summer. These versatile 1-day wonders are great for mass plantings, especially along walls or banks, or in combination with shrubs and trees. Use daylilies as accent plantings around foundations or with groundcovers.

Once established, daylilies spread quickly to form dense, broad clumps. Although you can leave the plants in place for years, some varieties produce so many stalks that the flowers get too crowded if the clumps aren't divided every 3 years or so. Lift the entire clump in late summer, pull or cut the thick tangled roots apart, and replant. ❈

HEUCHERA
(Alumroot, Coral Bells)

Heuchera 'Palace Purple'

THIS GROUP OF perennials is made up of lovely foliage plants, many of which also have showy flowers. The evergreen leaves of heuchera are rounded, heart-shaped, or triangular and have long slender leafstalks. The white, pink, or red flowers hang daintily in clusters from the leafstalks.

Plant these versatile perennials in containers, in rock or woodland gardens, as groundcovers, or in a mixed border. The flower clusters add an airy look to summer beds and borders, and the mounds of green foliage are excellent for edging. Make the most of heuchera leaves by pairing them with bright flowers, like red pansies.

Prolong heuchera bloom by removing the spent flowerstalks at the base of the plants. As heucheras grow, they produce woody crowns. Divide the crowns every 3 or 4 years in spring or fall.

In warm regions, provide shade from the hot afternoon sun to keep the leaves from bleaching. ❋

PLANT PARTICULARS

Zones: 3 to 9

Height: 1 to 3 feet

Spread: 12 to 18 inches

Shape: Mounds of leaves with taller flower spikes

Color: White, pink, or red flowers; green to dark red leaves

Bloom time: Spring, summer

Light needs: Full sun to partial shade

Soil: Rich; moist but well drained

HOSTA
(Hosta, Plantain Lily)

Hosta 'Thomas Hoag' and *H. undulata*

PLANT PARTICULARS

Zones: 3 to 8

Height: 6 inches to 3 feet

Spread: Varies by species

Shape: Wide mounds of leaves with taller flower spikes

Color: Lilac, white, or purple flowers; green, yellow, blue-green, and/or cream leaves

Bloom time: Summer to fall

Light needs: Light to full shade

Soil: Average to rich; moist

THE BOLD, DRAMATIC foliage of hostas is perfect for brightening up a shady area of your landscape. Their leafy clumps vary greatly in size, and come in a range of colors from deep green through chartreuse, yellow, and gold to blue. Leaves are oval, heart-shaped, or lance-shaped with smooth or wavy edges. Some varieties even produce spiky bloom stalks with white, lilac, or purple flowers.

Plant hostas with ferns, wildflowers, and other shade-loving perennials on the north side of your house or under the canopy of large trees. Or, interplant them with ferns and wild ginger for a beautiful shady groundcover. You can also plant them with early spring bulbs. The hostas will unfurl their leaves just when the bulb foliage starts to look shabby.

Hostas grow slowly and may take 2 to 4 years to reach their full size. Allow plenty of room when you plant them to accommodate for their mature size. Small varieties spread three times as wide as they are tall. Medium-sized varieties spread twice their height, and the large ones are at least as wide as they are tall. ❈

Iberis sempervirens 'Snowflake'

LOVELY LONG-FLOWERING perennials are a must for the spring garden. And that includes perennial candytuft (*I. sempervirens*), which offers tidy mounds of evergreen leaves that are covered in flat clusters of white flowers in early spring.

Candytuft is the consummate edging plant. Its low and compact growth, early flowers, and evergreen foliage make it perfect for planting along stairs or walks, or in the front of a bed or border. In rock gardens, combine candytuft with spring bulbs, bleeding hearts, rock cresses, and purple rock cress. In a border, plant it with tulips, columbines, forget-me-nots, and spring bulbs. Planted in raised beds or atop retaining walls, it can cascade over the side.

After the plants have bloomed for the season, cut them back by about one-third to remove the spent flowers to encourage compact growth and good foliage. Prune them hard, at least two-thirds back, every 2 to 3 years to encourage new stem growth and to promote flower production. These plants seldom need division. ❀

PLANT PARTICULARS

Zones: 2 to 9

Height: 3 to 12 inches

Spread: Varies by species

Shape: Low creeping mats

Color: White flowers; shiny evergreen leaves

Bloom time: Early spring

Light needs: Full sun to light shade

Soil: Average; well drained

IRIS
(Iris)

Iris siberica (Siberian iris)

PLANT PARTICULARS

Zones: 2 to 10

Height: 4 inches to 4 feet

Spread: Varies by species

Shape: Upright spiky clumps

Color: White, yellow, orange, brown, pink, purple, or blue flowers; green leaves

Bloom time: Spring, summer

Light needs: Full sun to light shade

Soil: Varies widely by species

AN IRIS EXISTS for every garden situation: sun or shade, moist or dry soil, early or late bloom. In addition, you're sure to find a color to suit your taste, because bloom colors include white, pink, red, purple, blue, yellow, and brown. You can choose from a host of different species, which include bearded irises, Siberian irises, reticulated irises, and yellow flag irises. Different species bloom at different times from winter through summer, so you can enjoy this perennial practically year-round. Many irises are excellent for cutting.

Bearded and Siberian irises are well suited to beds and borders with spring and early-summer perennials. Combine their strap-shaped foliage with peonies, hostas, cranesbills, and columbines. Plant moisture-loving yellow flag irises with ferns, hostas, and other lush perennials along the sides of ponds. Smaller iris species are perfect in rock gardens or at the front of a border.

If you want to divide your irises, do so after they've finished flowering in summer or early fall. Replant them immediately. ✽

LIATRIS
(Gayfeather, Blazing-Star)

Liatris spicata 'Kobold'

PLANT SOME OF these perennials, and you're sure to attract butterflies, which love the upright, fuzzy spikes and profusion of small red-violet to purple flowers. The spikes of gayfeathers open from the top down, unlike those of most other spike-flowering perennials, which open from the bottom up.

These native American perennials are a natural choice for meadow gardens, prairie plantings, and borders. In a border, combine them with yarrows, purple coneflowers, artemisias, Shasta daisies, garden phlox, and ornamental grasses. If you want to tone down pinkish purple varieties, pair them with silvery lamb's-ears. To jazz them up, plant them with coreopsis or yellow coneflower. And don't forget to include gayfeathers in your cutting garden; they're great for fresh-flower arrangements.

You don't need a green thumb to grow gayfeathers because they're tough, low-maintenance, long-lived perennials. If you leave them alone, they'll form large clumps; if you want to create new plants, divide the clumps in the fall. 🌼

PLANT PARTICULARS

Zones: 3 to 9

Height: 6 inches to 3 feet

Spread: 18 to 24 inches

Shape: Clumps of upright flowerstalks

Color: Purple, pink, or white flowers; green leaves

Bloom time: Summer

Light needs: Full sun

Soil: Average to rich; well drained

LILIUM
(Lily)

Lilium citronella

PLANT PARTICULARS

Zones: 2 to 9

Height: 1 to 7 feet

Spread: Varies by species

Shape: Tall, slender stalks topped with a cluster of flowers

Color: White, yellow, orange, red, or pink flowers; green leaves

Bloom time: Spring, summer

Light needs: Full sun to partial shade

Soil: Average; well drained

THIS LARGE GROUP of plants offers such a wide range of sizes, colors, and shapes that you're sure to find some to suit your garden. These perennials grow from bulbs that lack the papery brown covering (tunic) of bulbs such as tulips and daffodils. From the center of the bulb rises a tall stalk, which is clothed in leaves that may be narrow and grasslike, or wide and more swordlike. Nodding or upright flowers may be trumpet-, star-, or bowl-shaped. Lilies are available in various bloom colors, many of which have dark spots or streaks on the petals.

Combine lilies with baby's breath, hostas, asters, and other bushy perennials that will hide the bases of the lily stems. Or, plant generous groupings with ornamental grasses and vines.

If you plant tall lilies, you'll probably need to stake them. Insert a stake near the stem, taking care not to spear the bulb when you put the stake in the ground. Tie the stem loosely to the stake (see "Plant Supports" on page 11 for more tips on staking tall plants). ❈

LOBELIA
(Lobelia)

Lobelia cardinalis (cardinal flower)

HUMMINGBIRDS LOVE THESE perennials, particularly *L. cardinalis*, or cardinal flower. (Butterflies love them, too.) Lobelias produce erect spikes of irregularly shaped tubular flowers that come in many colors including blue and pink.

Lobelias are best suited to gardens with moist soil, especially along ponds and streams. They are good border plants, as long as the soil doesn't dry out. Plant them in the company of Siberian and Japanese irises, astilbes, ferns, and bold foliage plants such as hostas. Combine them with other moisture-tolerant border perennials such as daylilies, spiderworts, garden phlox, and sneezeweed. Great blue lobelia (*L. siphilitica*) has subtle blue flowers that mix well with goldenrods and ornamental grasses.

Although they tend to be short-lived, lobelias can produce many seedlings for transplanting; remove the flower spikes after blooming if you want to prevent self-sowing. Divide clumps in early fall to help plants perform well for several seasons. ❂

PLANT PARTICULARS

Zones: 2 to 9

Height: 2 to 4 feet

Spread: 1 to 2 feet

Shape: Erect spikes

Color: Red, purple, blue, white, or pink flowers; green leaves

Bloom time: Summer, fall

Light needs: Full sun to partial shade

Soil: Rich; constantly moist

LUPINUS
(Lupine)

Lupinus spp.

PLANT PARTICULARS

Zones: 2 to 7

Height: 18 inches to 5 feet

Spread: 1 to 2 feet

Shape: Mounds of leaves with tall flower spikes

Color: White, pink, purple, blue, or red flowers; green leaves

Bloom time: Spring, summer

Light needs: Full sun to light shade

Soil: Rich; moist but well drained

THESE PERENNIALS ARE a good choice for zones where summers are cool. (Lupines suffer in hot temperatures.) Lupines' tall, dense flower spikes produce pea-shaped flowers that come in shades of white, pink, purple, blue, and red.

Plant lupines for early summer color in cottage gardens and meadow gardens. Use them as an accent with flowering shrubs or in a border with irises, peonies, bellflowers, Oriental poppies, and annuals. They also make a wonderful accent in groundcovers such as common periwinkle.

Cut off spent flower spikes to promote possible regrowth, or let the seeds mature so plants can self-sow. For propagation, separate sideshoots from the clumps in fall. Or, if you aren't looking for a specific color (lupine seeds usually are sold in packets of mixed colors), sow seed in pots outdoors in late summer or indoors in winter. (Soaking the seed in warm water overnight can speed germination.) Place flats of seeds sown indoors in a refrigerator for 4 to 6 weeks before moving to a warm place. ❀

Monarda 'Squaw'

PUT OUT THE welcome mat for bees, butterflies, and hummingbirds with generous clumps of bee balm. This perennial has round heads of tightly packed flowers and aromatic leaves that add a splash of color to the landscape. Combine bee balms with lilies, phlox, yarrows, cranesbills, and astilbes. *M. didyma*, a wild species of bee balm, works well in the moist wild garden among bonesets, queen-of-the-prairie, hibiscus, and ferns.

Many bee balms are prone to powdery mildew, a fungal disease that appears as a dusty white coating on leaves and stems (see "Diseases That Affect Perennials" on page 39 for more information about how to recognize and prevent fungal infection). Help avoid powdery mildew problems by planting resistant varieties, such as bright pink 'Marshall's Delight'; choosing a site with good air circulation; and thinning bee balm stems as needed.

Bee balms spread rather quickly, so you'll probably want to divide the clumps every 2 or 3 years (in spring or fall) to keep them from taking over. Relocate the new transplants, or share them with friends. ❄

PLANT PARTICULARS

Zones: 3 to 9

Height: 1 to 4 feet

Spread: 3 feet

Shape: Spreading patches of upright stems

Color: Red, pink, white, purple, or yellow-green flowers; green leaves

Bloom time: Summer

Light needs: Full sun to partial shade

Soil: Rich; moist

NEPETA
(Catmint)

Nepeta mussinii (mauve catmint)

PLANT PARTICULARS

Zones: 3 to 8

Height: 1 to 2 feet

Spread: Varies by species

Shape: Soft, sprawling mounds

Color: Violet to lavender-blue flowers; gray-green leaves

Bloom time: Spring, early summer

Light needs: Full sun to light shade

Soil: Average; well drained

THIS PERENNIAL IS simply one of the best edging plants. Its misty mounds of soft gray-green leaves and wiry stems crowned with clusters of violet to lavender-blue flowers are lovely in the garden. Catmint also offers a long season of bloom—about 2½ months.

Plant catmint along walks, as an edging for beds, as a groundcover, or in a rock garden. The gray-green leaves and lavender-blue flowers look great with pale yellow coreopsis or yarrow, or with bright yellow evening primroses and daylilies. It also works well in front of peonies and roses.

Deer and rabbits seem to avoid catmint, so try planting it as a barrier to keep these critters away from plants they do love.

After the first flush of bloom, shear off the spent flower heads to promote rebloom (they'll quickly grow back again). To propagate catmint, dig up, divide, and transplant rooted stems. ✵

Paeonia 'Heritage'

PEONIES ARE PRIZED for their variety of form and color, exceptional hardiness, and ease of care. They can have single, semidouble, or double blooms that range in color from white, cream, and yellow to pink, rose, and scarlet.

A row of peonies can make a glorious early-summer hedge. Mix several varieties (with different bloom times) together to extend the bloom season as long as possible. Classic companions include irises, foxgloves, and columbines. Hosta foliage and pink peonies make a pretty combination that's also practical: The hostas serve as natural support for the floppy peonies.

Speaking of support, taller peonies and those with double flowers usually need staking to keep their blooms out of the mud. Use hoop stakes or straight stakes and string to support floppy stalks. Single-flowered peonies generally have self-supporting stems that stand up to wind and rain. ❈

PLANT PARTICULARS

Zones: 2 to 8

Height: 1 to 5 feet

Spread: 30 to 36 inches

Shape: Loose, flower-topped mounds

Color: White, yellow, cream, pink, rose, and scarlet flowers; green leaves

Bloom time: Spring, early summer

Light needs: Full sun to light shade

Soil: Rich; moist

PAPAVER
(Poppy)

Papaver orientale 'Perry's White'

PLANT PARTICULARS

Zones: 2 to 7

Height: 1 to 3 feet

Spread: 2 feet

Shape: Loose clumps

Color: Orange, red, pink, white, or yellow flowers; dark green leaves

Bloom time: Spring, early summer

Light needs: Full sun

Soil: Rich; well drained

THESE DELIGHTFUL FLOWERS are wonderful for adding vibrant color to your beds. Their crepe paper-like petals come in shades of orange, red, pink, white, or yellow. The flowers sit atop stout stems and open from nodding buds.

To get the most eye-popping color, plant the orange-scarlet, black-centered Oriental poppy (*P. orientale*). Bushy perennials that bloom after early summer, such as Russian sage and boltonia, make good companions. Other more subtle perennials that work well paired with bold-colored poppies include speedwells, bellflowers, baptisias, and blue stars. Use long-blooming cranesbills, perennial salvia, or spreading baby's breath to fill in the gaps after the poppies have finished flowering.

Rejuvenate crowded clumps (probably only once every 5 or 6 years) by dividing the plants just as the new leaves emerge in late summer. Lifted plants will invariably leave behind a few broken roots, which will grow into new plants. To propagate, take root cuttings while you're dividing the clumps. ❈

PENSTEMON
(Penstemon, Beardtongue)

Penstemon 'Alice Hindley'

TO BRING A touch of wildflowers to your beds, try penstemon. It produces slender, single-branched spikes with tiers of irregularly shaped flowers. The flowers vary in color from white to pink, rose, lavender, and violet. This airy-looking plant has lush rosettes of evergreen leaves that form wide patches and make attractive groundcovers when the plants aren't in bloom.

Use penstemon in container plantings, as an edging, as a groundcover, in a mixed border, or in a rock garden. Combine it with cranesbills, spiderworts, yarrows, evening primroses, lamb's-ears, yuccas, and ornamental grasses.

Success with penstemon depends on choosing the right species for your growing conditions. Species native to the western mountains, for example, often cook in the heat of midwestern gardens and rot in the humidity and dampness of eastern gardens. However, many excellent eastern natives and other adaptable species are available. Good drainage is essential for all varieties except *P. digitalis*, which tolerates moist soil. ❀

PLANT PARTICULARS

Zones: 2 to 9

Height: 4 inches to 3 feet

Spread: Varies by species

Shape: Tall spikes

Color: White, pink, rose, lavender, or violet flowers; evergreen leaves

Bloom time: Early summer through fall

Light needs: Full sun to partial shade

Soil: Average; very well drained

PEROVSKIA
(Russian Sage)

Perovskia atriplicifolia 'Blue Spire'

PLANT PARTICULARS

Zones: 4 to 9

Height: 3 to 5 feet

Spread: 2 to 4 feet

Shape: Airy, shrublike mound

Color: Powder blue flowers; gray-green leaves

Bloom time: Summer

Light needs: Full sun

Soil: Average; well drained to dry

THIS TOUGH, TROUBLE-FREE perennial laughs at heat, drought, and pests. Its shrubby, branching habit supports gray-green leaves and airy sprays of tiny powder blue flowers. In addition to being tough, Russian sage earns its keep year-round by producing soft shoots in spring, flowers that bloom for more than a month in summer, and seedheads that dry in fall for winter interest.

The soft blue flowers of Russian sage complement pink, yellow, deep blues, and purples. Plant it in the middle or back of the perennial border with yarrows, phlox, balloon flowers, gayfeathers, and ornamental grasses. Also, try it as a low-maintenance landscape feature or as an accent in a cottage garden.

Cut the woody stems of this plant down to about 1 foot in late fall or early spring to promote new growth. In the North, plants often die back to the soil but resprout from the roots. Russian sage seldom needs dividing. ❈

Phlox paniculata 'Snow Hare'

THEY'RE FAVORITES AMONG perennial gardeners, and rightly so. Phlox are easy to grow, bloom prolifically, and produce a heady fragrance. Depending on the variety, phlox may produce tall, leafy stems crowned with dense, domed heads of five-petaled flower clusters, or short, creeping stems that form an attractive groundcover.

One variety gardeners prefer is garden phlox (*P. paniculata*). Its mounded flower clusters combine well with other summer bloomers. Place garden phlox in the middle or rear of the garden, and give it ample room to spread. Combine it with perennials such as bonesets, bee balms, Shasta daisy, astilbes, meadowsweets, cranesbills, delphiniums, daylilies, and ornamental grasses.

To help prevent powdery mildew, choose a site with good air circulation, thin the stems of dense clumps, and water the plants from below to avoid wetting their leaves. 🕸

PLANT PARTICULARS

Zones: 2 to 9

Height: 4 inches to 5 feet

Spread: 24 to 30 inches

Shape: Varies among species

Color: White, pink, rose, red, violet, blue, or bicolored flowers; dark green leaves

Bloom time: Spring, summer

Light needs: Full sun to full shade

Soil: Varies among species

PLATYCODON
(Balloon flower)

Platycodon grandiflora (dwarf balloon flower)

PLANT PARTICULARS

Zones: 3 to 8

Height: 1 to 3 feet

Spread: 24 inches

Shape: Loose clumps

Color: Blue, pink, or white flowers; green leaves

Bloom time: Summer

Light needs: Full sun to light shade

Soil: Average to rich; well drained

PLANT IT NOW; enjoy it forever. A real showstopper, balloon flower flaunts star-shaped flowers that open from inflated round buds that resemble balloons.

These blooms look lovely with bright or pastel flowers and green or silvery foliage plants. Combine them with summer-blooming perennials such as yellow yarrows, alliums, violet sage, bee balms, and garden phlox. Use silvery foliage, such as lamb's-ears and artemisias, along with ornamental grasses to set off the bright flowers. Enjoy the blooms indoors as well as out; they last long as fresh-cut flowers if you singe the stem ends with a match to stop the milky sap from flowing.

The new shoots of balloon flowers are slow to emerge in spring, so be sure to mark their location so you don't dig into their clumps by mistake. The plants bloom for a month or more; removing the spent flowers will encourage the plants to continue blooming as well as keep them looking neat. ❈

POLYGONATUM

(Solomon's Seal)

Polygonatum biflorum

FOR THE AREAS of your garden in deep shade, try Solomon's seal. This graceful, arching plant has broad oval leaves and bell-shaped greenish or white flowers that hang below the foliage. In summer, it produces waxy, blue-black berries; in fall, the foliage turns yellow-brown.

Use Solomon's seal as edging, in a rock or a woodland garden, or at the back of a bed or a border. Combine it with bold foliage plants such as hostas, ferns, alumroots, wild ginger, and lady's-mantle. Most species will also do well under mature shade trees.

Although Solomon's seal prefers moist, rich soil, it will tolerate dry, stony soil. Divide plants whenever they start to outgrow their boundaries. To propagate, divide clumps in spring or fall and replant into amended soil. Or, remove the seeds from the berries in fall and immediately plant the seeds outdoors. (The seeds may take 2 years to germinate, and seedlings will grow slowly.)

PLANT PARTICULARS

Zones: 3 to 9

Height: 1 to 3 feet

Spread: 1 to 2 feet

Shape: Arching stems with dangling flowers

Color: Greenish or white flowers; green or variegated leaves that turn yellow-brown in fall

Bloom time: Spring

Light needs: Partial to full shade

Soil: Rich; moist

PRIMULA
(Primrose)

Primula japonica (Japanese primrose)

PLANT PARTICULARS

Zones: 2 to 8

Height: 2 inches to 2 feet

Spread: Varies by species

Shape: Rosettes of leaves with taller flowering stems or open, branched clusters

Color: Yellow, white, pink, purple, or red flowers; green leaves

Bloom time: Very early spring, early summer

Light needs: Full sun to partial shade

Soil: Rich; moist

PERKY PRIMROSES HAVE a place in every garden (they perform well in containers, too). These beloved five-petaled spring flowers bloom with flowering bulbs when the earth is reawakening, so plant them in clumps or drifts with spring bulbs such as tulips, snowdrops, and daffodils.

Some primrose varieties produce a tall stem, whereas others sport open, branched clusters close to the ground. Japanese primroses (*P. japonica*) love a spot with dependably damp soil, so combine them with irises, hostas, ferns, and lady's-mantle. If you live in a northern USDA plant hardiness zone that has erratic snowfall, mulch or cover your primroses for the winter to help them survive. In the South, provide consistent moisture and shade from the hot afternoon sun in summer; if the plants get too hot or dry, they will go dormant early—meaning you lose out on bloom time. ❊

Pulmonaria rubra

SOME LUNGWORT VARIETIES do double duty: They not only produce pretty flowers in early spring but also sport showy silver-spotted leaves that make a bold statement the rest of the year. Some varieties of these low-growing plants have flowers that do a mid-bloom costume change: They open pink and turn to blue.

Combine lungworts with daffodils and other spring bulbs in a bed or a border or under flowering trees or shrubs. The tough and attractive summer foliage is outstanding as a groundcover. In the perennials garden, plant lungworts in drifts with hellebores, anemones, bleeding hearts, and irises. And planted singly or in groups, they brighten up shady spots under trees and shrubs.

Once lungworts are established, they are fairly drought-tolerant. However, they'll go dormant early if the soil dries out. Divide overgrown clumps after flowering or in fall, and replant into amended soil. ❋

PLANT PARTICULARS

Zones: 2 to 8

Height: 9 inches to 2 feet

Spread: 1 to 2 feet

Shape: Loose clumps

Color: Pink, blue, red, or white flowers; green or variegated leaves

Bloom time: Spring

Light needs: Partial to full shade

Soil: Rich; moist

RUDBECKIA
(Coneflower, Black-Eyed Susan)

Rudbeckia 'Goldsturm'

PLANT PARTICULARS

Zones: 3 to 9

Height: 18 inches to 2 feet

Spread: Varies by species

Shape: Broad clumps of stiff, branched stalks

Color: Orange or yellow flowers; green leaves

Bloom time: Summer

Light needs: Full sun to light shade

Soil: Average to rich; well drained

TOUGH, ADAPTABLE CONEFLOWERS are the perfect perennials to grow if your thumb is more brown than green. Their daisylike blooms have golden yellow petals and brown or green centers that are either domed or flat.

These plants are invaluable for adding bright, long-lasting color to perennial gardens. Plant them with other summer-blooming flowers such as purple coneflowers, Russian sage, garden phlox, sedums, bee balms, and ornamental grasses, such as blue oat grass. Coneflowers also make good, long-lasting cut flowers, so you can enjoy them indoors as well as out in your garden.

Pinch off spent flowers to promote rebloom, or let the seedheads form to add winter interest to your garden. To propagate, divide clumps in spring, or dig up self-sown seedlings. You can sow seed outdoors in spring or fall. ❋

SALVIA

(Salvia, Sage)

Salvia × *Superba* 'May Night'

LIKE CONEFLOWERS, THESE perennials are easy to grow and will tolerate a wide variety of conditions (although they typically prefer well-drained soil). These plants are mounded to shrubby mints with tubular blue, purple, red, or pink flowers and square stems. Many salvias also have aromatic foliage.

Spiky salvias are super mid-border or edging plants for sunny gardens. Their upright habit contrasts beautifully with mounded plants, such as cranesbills and threadleaf coreopsis. They also look great combined with yuccas, yarrows, sedums, coneflowers, daylilies, daisies, mums, and ornamental grasses.

Plant salvias in full sun or light shade; they'll get leggy and flop in too much shade. Overly rich or moist soils also encourage flopping. Cutting the spent flower stems off your salvias can promote a second bloom in late summer. In fall or early spring, cut the plants back to the ground. ❋

PLANT PARTICULARS

Zones: 3 to 10

Height: 1 to 4 feet

Spread: Varies by species

Shape: Mounded to shrubby

Color: Blue, purple, pink, or red flowers; silver-gray, green, or variegated leaves

Bloom time: Summer, fall

Light needs: Full sun to light shade

Soil: Average; well drained to dry

SCABIOSA
(Scabious, Pincushion Flower)

Scabiosa caucasica 'Fama'

PLANT PARTICULARS

Zones: 3 to 7

Height: 18 inches to 2 feet

Spread: Varies by species

Shape: Clumps with long flower stems

Color: Blue, pink, or white flowers; gray-green leaves

Bloom time: Summer

Light needs: Full sun to light shade

Soil: Rich; well drained to dry

WANT THE PERFECT cutting flower? This old-fashioned perennial has fuzzy foliage and broad, flat flower heads with tiny, lacy flowers on tall stems. What's more, it blooms for a long time. The quaint look of pincushion flower makes it a charming addition to cottage gardens and informal borders. Daylilies, yarrows, and coreopsis are wonderful companions. Blue pincushion flowers and yellow heliopsis make a great pair, both in the garden and cut for indoor arrangements. To create a significant display of pincushion flowers, plant them together in groups of three or more.

Pincushion flowers will form good-sized clumps under ideal conditions but are sensitive to heat and excess soil moisture. If you live in a southern zone, place these plants where they will be shaded in the afternoon. Remove spent flowers to keep plants looking neat and encourage repeat blooms. Divide clumps in spring only if they become overcrowded. ✺

Sedum 'Joyce Henderson'

THICK, SUCCULENT, WAXY leaves and fleshy, often trailing stems make these perennials drought-tolerant plants. Sedums come in lots of shapes and sizes, providing interesting foliage and yellow, pink, or white showy flowers with little or no fuss. Plus, the seedheads of many varieties retain their color after flowering and hold their form when dried.

'Autumn Joy' is one popular sedum variety that looks great in several seasons. Its neat mounds are topped with green buds that open to reddish pink flowers in late summer. The flower heads hold their shape well into winter. Sedums are versatile plants for beds, borders, and rock gardens and as groundcovers under open trees. The low, spreading species works well along paths.

All sedums are tough, low-maintenance plants. Once established, they generally won't require much care from you. Just divide them in spring or fall to control their spread. ❈

PLANT PARTICULARS

Zones: 3 to 9

Height: 2 inches to 2 feet

Spread: 12 to 18 inches

Shape: Spreading mats to upright clumps

Color: Yellow, pink, or white flowers; green, red, yellow, or silver leaves

Bloom time: Spring, summer

Light needs: Full sun to partial shade

Soil: Average; well drained to dry

SOLIDAGO
(Goldenrod)

Solidago 'Laurin'

PLANT PARTICULARS

Zones: 3 to 9

Height: 1 to 5 feet

Spread: Varies by species

Shape: Clumps of upright stalks

Color: Yellow flowers; green leaves

Bloom time: Late summer, fall

Light needs: Full sun

Soil: Average; moist but well drained

GOLDENRODS ARE A welcome sight in the garden, blooming at a time when many other flowers are going dormant for the season. The lemon yellow or golden flowers are carried in spikelike, flat-topped, or plume-like clusters; the leafy stems may be smooth or hairy.

These easy-care perennials look as good in beds and borders as they do in meadows and wildflower gardens. Combine them with coneflowers, balloon flowers, gayfeathers, bonesets, lavender, sages, asters, and ornamental grasses. Most species of goldenrod prefer average soil (rich soils cause rampant spread and cause the flowers to flop over). All species of goldenrod hold up well under drought conditions.

Regardless of whether you choose to include goldenrod in your perennial garden, rest assured that goldenrods aren't responsible for your fall hay fever. They're mistakenly blamed for the irritating pollen that's produced by ragweed. Because goldenrod pollen isn't released into the wind (the plants are pollinated by insects), it can't be blamed for upper respiratory tract allergies. ❇

Stachys byzantina

DELIGHTFUL LAMB'S-EARS are extremely versatile in any landscape. Their soft, fuzzy leaves just beg to be touched, and their tiny flowers add an accent of color to the silvery foliage.

Use them at the front of a border or an herb garden—or along a path, where you'll brush by them frequently. Their foliage and flower spikes are a perfect complement to green leaves and both bright and pastel flowers. Plant lamb's-ears in formal or informal gardens with irises, goat's beards, alumroots, bergenias, and lungworts.

In hot, humid conditions, the leaves may die back because the woolly foliage traps water and encourages rot. If this happens, cut the leaves and stems to the ground; new foliage should sprout when things cool off. Also, you can cut the flower stems to the ground after bloom to keep the plants looking tidy.

All species of lamb's-ears spread well when grown in the conditions they like best. Divide and replant overgrown clumps in the fall to control their spread, if you wish. ❊

PLANT PARTICULARS

Zones: 2 to 8

Height: 6 inches to 2 feet

Spread: 1 foot

Shape: Spreading mats with upright flower stems

Color: Purple, pink, or white flowers; silver-gray leaves

Bloom time: Spring, summer

Light needs: Full sun to light shade

Soil: Varies among species

VERBENA
(Verbena, Vervain)

Verbena spp.

PLANT PARTICULARS

Zones: 4 to 10

Height: 4 inches to 5 feet

Spread: 1 foot

Shape: Varies among species

Color: Pink, purple, white, or blue flowers; green leaves

Bloom time: Summer

Light needs: Full sun to light shade

Soil: Average; well drained to dry

THE POPULARITY OF these perennials stems from their different shapes, from tall upright plants to low, creeping, mat-forming ones. Surely, at least one variety will work well in your landscape. The brightly colored flowers have five flat petals that are carried in flat or spiky clusters on top of wiry stems.

The mat-forming varieties are excellent for tying together mixed plantings. Let them creep among foliage plants such as yuccas, artemisias, mulleins, and ornamental grasses. They also serve to fill in gaps between tall flowering perennials such as coneflowers, butterfly weeds, and yarrows. Contrary to usual practice, plant upright varieties at the front of a border, because the verbenas' tall, airy stems will allow you to see the plants behind.

These tough, heat- and drought-tolerant perennials bloom tirelessly throughout the summer. The creeping varieties spread quickly to form showy groundcovers, whereas the upright varieties spread slowly. ❋

VERONICA

(Veronica, Speedwell)

Veronica austriaca 'Shirley Blue'

DEPENDABLE, LONG-BLOOMING speedwells are available in both upright and creeping varieties. The blooms are spikes of small flowers in shades of white, pink, rose, purple, and blue. Speedwells' leaves may be narrow and lance-shaped, oblong, oval, or wedge-shaped.

Practically maintenance-free, speedwells are very heat- and drought-tolerant—perfect for beds, borders, and rock gardens. You can also use them as edging, in a wildflower meadow, or along a path. Combine their colorful spiky flowers with mounded plants such as coreopsis, butterfly weeds, yarrows, cranesbills, daylilies, and ornamental grasses.

Pinch off the dead flower spikes to keep the plants blooming, and divide the plants in spring or fall for propagation or to control spread. (The creeping types tend to spread quite widely, so watch them carefully, or you may end up with plants in unwanted areas—like your neighbor's yard.)

PLANT PARTICULARS

Zones: 3 to 8

Height: 4 inches to 6 feet

Spread: Varies among species

Shape: Varies among species

Color: White, pink, purple, or blue flowers; green leaves

Bloom time: Spring, summer

Light needs: Full sun to light shade

Soil: Average to rich; moist but well drained

Your Seasonal Perennial-Care Calendar

THIS MONTH-BY-MONTH calendar is a handy reference guide to help you create and maintain your perennial garden. When using the calendar, keep in mind that these are only general guidelines. What you do specifically in your beds each month depends on what your climate and growing season are like (and that depends on what USDA Plant Hardiness Zone you live in—see page 106).

JANUARY

Just because it's winter doesn't mean your landscape has to be bare and boring. Here are some things you can do this year to perk up your landscape for next winter.

- Go outside and take a **look at your perennial garden** (or where you'd like to put perennials).

- Are there places where shrubs, ornamental grasses, or plants with interesting **winter seed pods** might add structure and improve your garden's winter appearance?

- If so, make a list of those plants—or put your thoughts on paper in the form of a winter **garden design** to refer to later.

FEBRUARY

Read perennial gardening books and catalogs for ideas about what you want to plant and for design suggestions. **Order new plants** and seeds from mail-order catalogs now. Start counting down the days until **spring** is scheduled to arrive in your zone.

MARCH

Clean up existing perennial garden beds. **Rake out** fallen **leaves** and winter mulch as spring growth begins, adding the leaves and mulch to your compost pile so it doesn't go to waste. When the soil is dry enough to dig, **prepare new garden areas**, amending the soil with compost.

APRIL

The arrival of spring means there's plenty for you to do to get ready for a new season of growing perennials.

- **Cut back woody perennials** such as Russian sage and butterfly bush as they begin to show new growth.

- **Begin a garden journal**; note what plants are in bloom when, what you like and don't like, and what ideas you have for changing things.

- Don't rely on **plant labels** to remember where everything is and what it is. (Plant labels have a habit of disappearing over time.) Instead, **make a garden plan** on paper or on your computer, if you don't already have one, and keep it updated as your garden evolves.

MAY

Now you can really start to go to town in your beds. **Dig up and divide** summer- and fall-blooming plants, and share some of your divisions with family and friends. Plant perennials, and after danger

Winter

Spring

Summer

Fall

of **frost** has passed, fill in empty spots with annuals for all-season **colorful bloom.**

JUNE

Mulch the perennial garden with compost, chopped leaves, or **shredded bark** to help control weeds. Add new plants as desired. Continue to keep a detailed journal, noting any problem spots in your garden.

JULY

During these dog days of summer:

- **Watch for signs of pests** or disease, and research organic ways to prevent them in the first place.

- **Look through mail-order catalogs** for disease resistant varieties to replace problem plants next spring.

- **Water your garden** during dry spells.

- Keep things looking neat by **weeding** and deadheading **regularly**.

- **Cut back plants** that have finished blooming to promote new growth.

- **Cut perennials** to use in fresh-flower bouquets and arrangements indoors.

AUGUST

Your late-season garden can still look great during this month; you just need to stay on top of things.

- **Take a good look** at your beds, noting colorless areas.

- **Research** possible substitutions, **relocations**, or additions and jot them down in your garden journal.

- The end of this month is a good time to **move or add plants**, particularly those that bloom in spring and early summer.

- **Dig up and divide** early-blooming plants, keeping the new divisions well watered until they become established.

SEPTEMBER

Take cuttings of tender plants (such as salvias) and root them in **moist perlite** for next year's garden. Prepare new peren-

nial beds. Amend the soil with compost; take a **soil test**, and adjust the pH if necessary. Cover the bare soil with a mulch of chopped leaves to **prevent erosion**.

OCTOBER

Clean up existing beds after the first **hard frost**, and throw the spent plants on your compost pile. Leave upright seedheads and pods in the garden for winter interest (the **birds** will thank you, too). Cover the beds with a 3- to 4-inch layer of mulch for winter protection.

NOVEMBER

Pot the now-rooted cuttings you took back in September and place them on a bright windowsill for the winter.

DECEMBER

Lay **evergreen boughs** over your perennials to provide an additional layer of insulation. Page through your garden journal and **dream** about the new perennials you'd like to try the next year.

Perennials Glossary

Learning the lingo that goes with growing perennials will make your trips to the garden center much easier. Here's a list of terms you're likely to come across in gardening books (including this one) and in the gardening aisles.

Acidic soil. Soil with a pH value lower than 7.0.

Alkaline soil. Soil with a pH value higher than 7.0.

Amendment. Material that improves soil condition and aids plant growth.

Annual. A plant that completes its life cycle in one growing season and then dies.

Biennial. A plant that completes its life cycle in 2 years and then dies.

Bulb. An underground stem that stores energy in modified leaves, as in the bulbs of daffodils or tulips.

Compost. Decomposed and partially decomposed organic matter that's dark in color and crumbly in texture. Used as a soil amendment, compost increases the water-holding capacity of sandy soil, improves the drainage of clay soil, and is an excellent nutrient source for microorganisms, which later release nutrients to your plants.

Corm. An underground stem that stores energy in modified stem tissue, as in a crocus stem.

Crown. The part of a plant where the stem meets the roots, usually at or just below the soil line.

Cultivar. Short for "cultivated variety." Any plant that's bred for specific characteristics, such as color, fragrance, disease resistance, or other desirable qualities.

Cutting. Removing a piece of stem or root from an existing plant to grow into a new plant.

Deadheading. Removing spent flowers from a growing plant.

Disbudding. Removing some of a plant's buds to encourage the remaining buds to grow larger.

Disk flowers. The small, tube-shaped blooms located in the center of the flowering heads of plants such as asters and daisies.

Division. A method of propagation by which a plant clump is separated or split apart into two or more plants.

Evergreen. A plant that keeps its green foliage through the winter.

Hardy (perennial). A perennial plant that tolerates frost.

Herbaceous. A plant that dies back to the ground each year; not woody.

Humus. A dark-colored, stable form of organic matter that remains after most of the plant and animal residues in it have decomposed; the organic component of soil.

Insecticidal soap. A specially formulated solution of fatty acids that kills insect pests such as aphids, mites, and whiteflies.

Life cycle. The germination, growth, flowering, seed production, and death of a plant.

Mulch. A layer of organic or inorganic material (such as shredded leaves, straw, bark, pine needles, lawn clippings, or black plastic) that's spread on the ground around plants to conserve soil moisture and discourage weeds. As organic mulches decompose, they help to build the soil.

Neutral soil. Soil with pH of 7.0—that is, neither acidic nor alkaline.

Perennial. A plant that flowers and sets seed for two or more seasons.

pH. A number from 1.0 to 14.0 that's a measure of the acidity or alkalinity: 7.0 is neutral, below 7.0 is acidic, and above 7.0 is alkaline. Soil pH greatly affects the availability of nutrients to plants.

Pinching. Removing the tips of stems to encourage more compact, bushier plants; prevent flopping; and ensure more bloom.

Propagate. To make new plants from existing ones. Some methods of propagation include saving seed from plants and then planting the seed, taking cuttings from plants, and dividing clumps of plants.

Rhizome. A horizontal underground stem modified and often enlarged for food storage.

Semiwoody. A perennial plant that forms woody stems but is less substantial than a shrub.

Succulent. Having thick, fleshy, water-holding leaves or stems.

Taproot. The central, often thickened root of a plant.

Tender (perennial). A perennial plant from a tropical or subtropical region that won't survive the winter outside in North America, except in subtropical regions such as Florida and southern California.

Terminal bud. The bud borne at the tip of a stem.

Thinning. Removing some stems of dense, bushy plants to let in light and improve air circulation, often to help prevent mildew on susceptible plants.

Tuber. A swollen, underground stem modified to store large quantities of food.

Variegated. Striped, spotted, or otherwise marked with a color other than green; often used to describe leaves.

Woody. A perennial plant such as a shrub or tree that doesn't die down to the ground each year.

Recommended Reading & Resources

Books & Periodicals

Ball, Jeff, and Liz Ball. *Rodale's Flower Garden Problem Solver*. Emmaus, PA: Rodale, 1990.

Bradley, Fern Marshall, ed. *Gardening with Perennials*. Emmaus, PA: Rodale, 1996.

Burrell, C. Colston. *Perennial Combinations*. Emmaus, PA: Rodale, 1999.

Clausen, Ruth Rogers, and Nicholas H. Ekstrom. *Perennials for American Gardens*. New York: Random House, 1989.

Cox, Jeff. *Perennial All-Stars*. Emmaus, PA: Rodale, 1998.

DiSabato-Aust, Tracy. *The Well-Tended Perennial Garden*. Portland, OR: Timber, 1998.

Harper, Pamela, and Frederick McGourty. *Perennials: How to Select, Grow, and Enjoy*. Los Angeles, CA: Price Stern Sloan, 1985.

McClure, Susan. *Easy-Care Perennial Gardens*. Emmaus, PA: Rodale, 1997.

Organic Gardening magazine. Rodale, 33 E. Minor Street, Emmaus, PA 18098.

Phillips, Ellen, and C. Colston Burrell. *Rodale's Illustrated Encyclopedia of Perennials*. Emmaus, PA: Rodale, 1993.

Powell, Eileen. *From Seed to Bloom: How to Grow over 500 Annuals, Perennials, and Herbs*. Pownal, VT: Storey, 1995.

Sombke, Laurence. *Beautiful Easy Flower Gardens*. Emmaus, PA: Rodale, 1995.

Taylor, Norman. *Taylor's Guide to Perennials*. Boston: Houghton Mifflin Co., 1986.

Sources of Perennials

André Viette Farm and Nursery
P.O. Box 1109
Fishersville, VA 22939
Phone: (800) 575-5538
Fax: (540) 934-0782
Web site: www.viette.com

Bluestone Perennials
7211 Middle Ridge Road
Madison, OH 44057
Phone/fax: (800) 852-5243
Web site: www.bluestoneperennials.com

Busse Gardens
17160 245th Avenue
Big Lake, MN 55309
Phone: (800) 544-3192
Fax: (320) 286-6601
Web site: www.bussegardens.com

Canyon Creek Nursery
3527 Dry Creek Road
Oroville, CA 95965
Phone: (530) 533-2166
Web site: www.canyoncreeknursery.com

Carroll Gardens
444 East Main Street
Westminster, MD 21157
Phone: (800) 638-6334
Fax: (410) 857-4112
Web site: www.carrollgardens.com

Forestfarm
990 Tetherow Road
Williams, OR 97544-9599
Phone: (541) 846-7269
Fax: (541) 846-7269
Web site: www.forestfarm.com

Gardens North
5984 Third Line Road N
North Gower, Ontario K0A 2T0
Phone: (613) 489-0065
Fax: (613) 489-1208
Web site: www.gardensnorth.com

Heronswood Nursery Ltd.
7530 N.E. 288th Street
Kingston, WA 98346-9502
Phone: (360) 297-4172
Fax: (360) 297-8321
Web site: www.heronswood.com

Kurt Bluemel, Inc.
2740 Greene Lane
Baldwin, MD 21013-9523
Phone: (800) 248-7584
Fax: (410) 557-9785
Web site: www.bluemel.com

Louisiana Nursery
5853 Highway 182
Opelousas, LA 70570
Phone: (318) 948-3696
Fax: (318) 942-6404
Web site: www.louisiananursery.com

Niche Gardens
1111 Dawson Road
Chapel Hill, NC 27516
Phone: (919) 967-0078
Fax: (919) 967-4026
Web site: www.nichegdn.com

Park Seed Company
1 Parkton Avenue
Greenwood, SC 29647-0001
Phone: (800) 845-3369
Fax: (800) 275-9941
Web site: www.parkseed.com

The Perennial Gardens
13139 224th Street
Maple Ridge, British Columbia V4R 2P6
Phone: (604) 467-4218
Fax: (604) 467-3181
Web site: www.perennialgardener.com

Plant Delights Nursery
9241 Sauls Road
Raleigh, NC 27603
Phone: (919) 772-4794
Fax: (919) 662-0370
Web site: www.plantdel.com

Plants of the Southwest
Agua Fria, Route 6, Box 11A
Santa Fe, NM 87501
Phone: (800) 788-7333
Fax: (505) 438-8800
Web site: www.plantsofthesouthwest.com

Siskiyou Rare Plant Nursery
2825 Cummings Road
Medford, OR 97501
Phone: (541) 772-6846
Fax: (541) 772-4917
Web site: www.wave.net/upg/srpn

Song Sparrow Perennial Farm
13101 East Rye Road
Avalon, WI 53505
Phone: (800) 553-3715
Fax: (608) 883-2257
E-mail: sparrow@jvlnet.com

Thompson & Morgan Inc.
P.O. Box 1308
Jackson, NJ 08527
Phone: (800) 274-7333
Fax: (888) 466-4769
Web site: www.thompson-morgan.com

Wayside Gardens
1 Garden Lane
Hodges, SC 29695-0001
Phone: (800) 845-1124
Fax: (800) 817-1124
Web site: www.waysidegardens.com

White Flower Farm
P.O. Box 50
Litchfield, CT 06759-0050
Phone: (800) 503-9624
Fax: (860) 496-1418
Web site: www.whiteflowerfarm.com

Acknowledgments

Contibutors to this book include C. Colston Burrell, Jill Jesiolowski Cebenko, Cheryl Long, Vicki Mattern, and Ellen Phillips.

Photo Credits

Matthew Benson 27

Jim Block vi, 4 (top), 11 (top), 14, 17, 19 (top), 20, 36 (top), 36 (bottom), 48, 49, 56, 58, 59, 61, 64, 66, 72, 76, 78, 89, 96-97

David Cavagnaro 84

Margery Daughtrey 39 (bottom), 40 (bottom), 41 (bottom)

Grace Davis 37 (bottom), 39 (top)

R. Todd Davis 53, 65, 71

Alan and Linda Detrick 11 (bottom), 16, 37 (middle), 38 (top), 40 (top), 41 (top), 46, 54, 62, 63, 73, 79

Bill Johnson 47, 90

Mitch Mandel 2, 8 (middle), 8 (bottom), 9 (top)

Alison Miksch 24

Clive Nichols cover, i, iv, 4 (bottom), 19 (bottom), 21 (bottom) 51, 52, 55, 57, 60, 67, 68, 69, 74, 75, 77, 80, 81, 82, 83, 87, 88, 91, 92, 93, 94, 95

Jerry Pavia 21 (top)

Daniel Proctor 6, 10 (top), 12, 26 (top), 28 (all), 29, 30, 34, 35, 44

Susan A. Roth 43 (bottom), 50, 70, 86

Michael S. Thompson 10 (bottom), 85

Chuck Weight 43 (top)

Ron West 38 (bottom)

judywhite 37 (top)

Kurt Wilson 8 (top), 9 (middle), 9 (bottom), 22, 26 (bottom), 31, 32, 33

Index

Primrose (*Primula* spp.), 21, 86, *86*
Primula spp., 21, 86, *86*
Pruning shears, 9, *9*
Pulmonaria spp., 18, 21, 42, 87, *87*
Purple coneflowers (*Echinacea* spp.),
   62, *62*

R

Rabbits, 43, *43,* 78
Rhizomes, defined, 5
Root rot, 40, *40*
Rudbeckia spp., 20, 88, *88*
Russian sage (*Perovskia* spp.), 3, 82, *82*
Rust, 41, *41*

S

Sages (*Salvia* spp.), 35, 42, 89, *89*
Salvia spp., 35, 42, 89, *89*
Sawdust
   as mulch, 13
   as soil amendment, 27
Scabiosa spp., 90, *90*
Seasonal care calendar, 96–97
Sedum spp., 18, 35, 91, *91*
Semiwoody perennials, defined, 3
Shade-tolerant plants, 21, *21*
Shape, as design consideration, 18–19, *19*
Shasta daisies (*Chrysanthemum* spp.), 56
Shopping, for plants, 22–23, *22*
Siberian iris *(Iris siberica),* 16, 19, 72, *72*
Site selection, 4–5, *4,* 15–16, 20–21,
   20, 21
Slugs, 37, *37,* 55
Snails, 37, *37*
Soaker hoses, 10, *10, 31*
Soil
   amending, 27, *27*
   testing, 25–26, *26*
   types, 25–26
Solidago spp., 20, 92, *92*
Solomon's seal (*Polygonatum* spp.), 18, 21,
   85, *85*
Spades, 8, *8*
Specimen plants, 16
Speedwell (*Veronica* spp.), 95, *95*
Spider mites, 38, *38*
Spurge (*Euphorbia* spp.), 20, 64, *64*

Stachys spp., 18, 20, 93, *93*
Straw
   as mulch, 13, 33
   as soil amendment, 27

T

Tender perennials, defined, 3
Texture, as design consideration,
   19, *19*
Thinning, 34
Thrips, 38, *38*
Tools
   quality, 7–8
   types, 8–11, *8, 9, 10, 11*
Trowels, 8, *8*
True bulbs, defined, 5
Tuberous roots, defined, 5
Tubers, defined, 5

U

USDA Plant Hardiness Zone Map, 3, *106*

V

Verbena spp., 94, *94*
Veronica spp., 95, *95*
Vervain (*Verbena* spp.), 94, *94*
Virginia bluebells *(Mertensia virginica),* 21

W

Watering cans, 10, *10*
Watering wands, 10
Water techniques, 31–32, *31*
Wax begonias, 3
Weeding, 2, 33–34, *33*
Wilt, 41, *41*
Windflowers (*Anemone* spp.), 48, *48*
Wood chips, as mulch, 13
Woody perennials, defined, 3
Wormwood (*Artemisia* spp.), 18, 20,
   35, 50, *50*

Y

Yarrow (*Achillea* spp.), *17,* 20, 35, 46, *46*
Yellow flag iris (*Iris* spp.), 72
Yucca (*Yucca* spp.), 18

USDA Plant Hardiness Zone Map

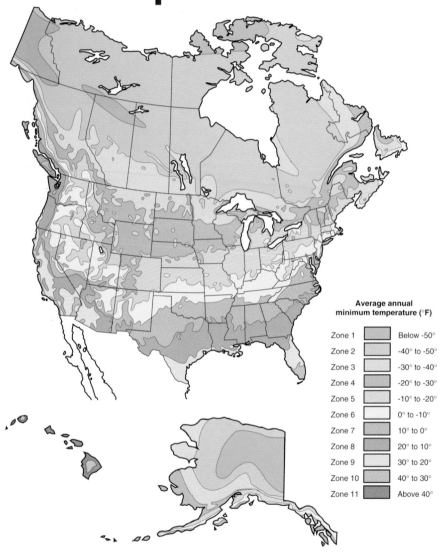

Average annual minimum temperature (°F)

Zone		Temperature
Zone 1		Below -50°
Zone 2		-40° to -50°
Zone 3		-30° to -40°
Zone 4		-20° to -30°
Zone 5		-10° to -20°
Zone 6		0° to -10°
Zone 7		10° to 0°
Zone 8		20° to 10°
Zone 9		30° to 20°
Zone 10		40° to 30°
Zone 11		Above 40°

This map was revised in 1990 and is recognized as the best indicator of minimum temperatures available. Look at the map to find your area, then match its color to the key. When you've found your color, the key will tell you what hardiness zone you live in. Remember that the map is a general guide; your particular conditions may vary.